792.8
Ne   Neale, Wendy
      On your toes:
      beginning ballet

DATE DUE			
MAY 2 9 1992			
OCT 2 1 1998			

On Your Toes

On Your Toes
Beginning Ballet

A COMPLETE GUIDE TO PROPER BALLET
TRAINING FOR PRE-KINDERGARTEN
TO ADULT BEGINNERS

by Wendy Neale

A HERBERT MICHELMAN BOOK

CROWN PUBLISHERS, INC.   NEW YORK

In memory of my parents

Copyright © 1980 by Wendy Neale
All rights reserved. No part of this book may be reproduced
or utilized in any form or by any means, electronic or mechanical,
including photocopying, recording, or by any information storage
and retrieval system, without permission in writing from the publisher.
Inquiries should be addressed to Crown Publishers, Inc.,
One Park Avenue, New York, New York 10016
Printed in the United States of America
Published simultaneously in Canada
by General Publishing Company Limited
Library of Congress Cataloging in Publication Data
Neale, Wendy.   On your toes.
"A Herbert Michelman book."
Includes index.
1.   Ballet—Study and teaching—United States.
2.   Ballet dancing.   3.   Ballet—Vocational
guidance.   I.   Title.
GV1788.5.N4   1980   792.8'0973   79–26336
ISBN: 0–517–532115
Design by Camilla Filancia
10   9   8   7   6   5   4   3   2   1
First edition

Contents

Acknowledgments

Thanks to Mr. Ben Sommers and Ms. Judy Weiss of Capezio and Mr. Fred Aaron of Frederick Freed, all in New York, who supplied the information necessary for the section on pointe shoes.

The Dance Research Department at Lincoln Center Public Library for the Performing Arts has been an invaluable source of information, for which I am sincerely grateful. I wish to say thank you particularly to the staff for their assistance, together with Rosanna Seravalli, Dance Faculty, Purchase College, SUNY, Purchase, New York, and Nicholas Grimaldi of the National Association for Regional Ballet.

Also to Dr. Rocco John La Manna, Senior Child Psychologist at Coney Island Hospital, who supplied most of the information on which Chapter Seven, "Keeping the Balance," is based, thanks—and to Dr. Albert Ellis, psychologist, quoted in the same chapter.

The most special thanks to all the teachers quoted in this book, who showed such particular concern for the problems dealt with herein and who took such care in answering the endless questions. They not only allowed their classes to be observed by the author at any time, but also accommodated Steven Caras when he needed to take photographs. For allowing an observer on days they must have felt that it was the last thing they wanted, very particular thanks also to the dancers and students themselves.

On Your Toes

The reader will notice that the personal pronoun "she" rather than "he" has been used throughout the book. This has been done simply because the majority of people in dance are female, and it is felt that the pronoun "one" is too formal to be used here. However, as such emphasis is now being put on encouraging boys to study dance, Chapter Eight "The Boy in Dance" has been devoted to them.

Introduction

Mayor Fiorello La Guardia remarked, "I'm a guy who likes to keep score. With ballet, I can't tell who's ahead." In the decades since he made this statement ballet has come a long way. Few people in public life today would want to acknowledge that they know less about dance and ballet than other forms of entertainment.

The thirst for dance has caused new ballet schools to spring up all over the United States. Since there is no certification for ballet teachers in this country, this is somewhat regrettable, for the majority of potential ballet students, or the parents of young aspirants, have no idea that a bad teacher can do a great deal of harm to a dancer's body.

Few people would take a Stradivarius violin to a model builder to be repaired, but that is a fair analogy. After years of bad training, that superior instrument—the body—may continue to look the same on the outside, but the minute the dancer tries to dance, what she produces might be physically the equivalent of the sound emitted by a badly overhauled violin. A student who submits herself to years of incompetent training considerably reduces her chances of becoming a dancer, and even healthy growth may be hampered.

From the age of eight, if a child shows signs of taking dance seriously, it is advisable to see that she is safely installed in a school that provides sound instruction to make sure her body develops correctly. If such development is not safeguarded, the repercussions can carry far beyond physical problems. When the time comes for her to apply to the major—even company—schools, she will find herself wholly unable to do the required steps correctly, and this, in turn, may cause severe emotional problems.

Possibly the best way to guard against being subjected to the incapable teacher is to contact the nearest company or school that has a good reputation. (See Chapter Six.)

With few exceptions, good instructors are located in the major cities, where they can attract the greatest number of pupils, and where they will also stand a chance of being able to train students who have some potential, rather than only those who could well have been cast in the "Dance of the Hours"* in Walt Disney's *Fantasia*.

One thing is definite. Nobody should walk into a dance school and simply enroll either herself or a child in a class without having first made sure of what she is entering into.

When a person first walks into a classroom there are certain observations to be made. They vary from the extremely positive to the equally negative. The aim of this book is to help the one who knows little or nothing about ballet classes to be able to make a judgment with some confidence.

---

* The ballet music from the opera *La Gioconda* by Amilcare Ponchielli. In Disney's film, the music was danced to by cartoon hippos and ostriches.

Ballet Class
THE FACILITY

The facility itself is a most important aspect of the ballet class and should be carefully scrutinized—from the floor, to the walls, to the ceiling.

Floor Materials and Pliability

As David Howard, a noted New York teacher, describes it, the floor should be made of wood and should be resilient. This is achieved by placing sleepers (heavy, horizontal timbers for distributing loads) underneath the surface. Many people make the mistake of putting tiles on concrete floors, which jar the back and cause severe injuries. Neither does it suffice to put wood on top of concrete, because such a layer cannot absorb the shock of the work that takes place in a ballet class. It is bad for one's anatomy even to walk on concrete a great deal, which is why runners buy specially designed, expensive shoes if they are running on concrete and yet wish to keep injuries to a minimum. In jumping, the body is designed to absorb a certain amount of shock, when the legs are bent in landing, but the surface on which the jumper lands must be able to absorb the rest. Since the human body was designed to walk on earth and sand, the trouble began when man's dwellings became sophisticated. However, there were probably fewer problems in the old buildings, before floors were made of concrete, and until man decided to stretch his anatomy to the limit and invented ballet.

Good wooden floors are expensive to install, which is the reason many studios do not have them. In old buildings, there is a chance the floor will be made of wood, since before the days of concrete that was the material used to construct virtually all floors. However, it does not mean because a dance school is in a new building the floors will not be good. It is possible to have a wooden floor constructed on top of concrete, as long as the wooden floor is raised high enough on sleepers to give it the necessary resilience.

On the assumption that for every positive there must be a negative, it can also be a disadvantage if a dancer becomes used to a floor that is too bouncy. Certainly a floor like this will not cause harm to the body, but it makes jumping considerably easier: with less effort the body will go higher into the air. Ultimately this can bring disappointment to the dancer who has practiced on a bouncy floor—when the time comes for her to dance on a harder floor. The feeling of losing one's jump can produce a terrible shock; clearly it is not a good idea to become so used to a floor with the spring of a trampoline that anything less presents problems. Also, it actually causes a delay in timing, which means that a dancer will not be able to fit her steps to the music correctly.

George Balanchine, Ballet Master of the New York City Ballet, spent many hours doing research with various woods at the time the New York State Theater, Lincoln Center, was being built, in order to develop floors that he felt would best be suited to the New York City Ballet. The result is that the company has floors and a stage that would be envied by any dancer.

Floor Surface

The surface of the floor should be smooth enough so a dancer's feet are able to glide across it when doing steps, although it is equally important for it not to be slippery. To help alleviate this situation, a dancer uses a substance called rosin* on the shoes, and the rosin box is a familiar sight in dance studios. However, as this substance builds up on the floor surface and becomes combined with the sweat of the dancers and the humidity of the room, it causes the floor surface to become sticky, at which stage it needs to be specially cleaned. On a

---

*"The translucent, brittle resin left after distilling the turpentine from the crude resin of the pine." (The Random House College Dictionary, Revised Edition, 1975).

Third-year class at the San Francisco Ballet School, in *passé*. Note
the spacious studio with its excellent wooden floor.
Photo: Fred Morales, Jr.

wooden floor, this can present problems, because it requires sanding
and resealing.

Having coped with this problem for some months, Douglas Wassell, associate teacher at the David Howard School of Ballet, talked of
the situation at David Howard's studio, where it was finally decided
to cover the wooden floor with battleship linoleum. This, said Mr.
Wassell, can be easily buffed about once a month in order to clean
the surface. It is done with a chemical, and the floor is not polished.

Battleship linoleum, although it is hard to obtain, is an ideal surface for dancers as long as the floor underneath is well sprung. In

fact, it is the surface used by major professional companies on stage. They carry their linoleum with them on tour, which guarantees that they have an even surface to dance on. Without it there can be problems. Anthony Dowell recalls times when he has danced on stages "that have surfaces like a plowed field."

A stage surface is cleaned with ammonia before every performance. If a principal requests it, Jerry Rice, Stage Manager of American Ballet Theatre, says the stagehands will clean it again during an intermission.

Marley flooring, a superior composition, is also used in studios and on stages, although dancers are not supposed to put rosin on their shoes when they work on it, since it destroys the surface.

Another substance that can be used to prevent slipping is a product called Slip-Nomor, though it is not adequate to preclude the use of rosin. In an emergency, where nothing else is available, even Coca-Cola comes in handy, since it is sticky when dry. At SUNY's Purchase College, Purchase, New York, some School of American Ballet students recently gave a performance of ballets choreographed by Jean-Pierre Bonnefous. Mr. Bonnefous requested that the refrigerators be raided for the popular drink, whereupon the stagehands rushed on stage with mop and bucket to swab the stage with it in an effort to counteract the slipperiness. The theater was basically ideal and the flooring was Marley, but by some mischance the dancers were reflected in it with the clarity of a lake, indicating that it had been polished, or at least well buffed. Polishing is obviously a treatment never to be given to dance floors.

Studio Size

The size of the floor is also significant. If a room is too small, the student will not be able to move freely when doing jumps or turns, for fear of bumping into the opposite wall. This will cause her to think more of how small to keep her steps so as to avoid bruises rather than concentrating on the quality of the steps themselves and being able to stretch out during the jumps. Barbara Thuesen, currently teaching in Ithaca, New York, feels this to be a serious problem. If the muscles are constantly tensing to keep the body movements short in order to cope with the confines of a small floor, they will eventually become bulky. If a muscle is to be developed properly, it must have the freedom to contract and stretch to its limits. Also, purely from the enjoyment point of view, it is much more exhilarating to be able to open out freely across a large floor rather than having to cramp one's way across a small one. Since purity of line and flow of movement are the essence of classical ballet, even a beginning student should be able to develop a feeling of open space, since she will have to become

Dennis Nahat teaching a class at the School of Cleveland Ballet, in a spacious, well-equipped studio. The students are in fifth position.

accustomed to it if she advances to the point where she is dancing onstage. Many new auditoriums have extremely large stages, having been built to accommodate everything from traveling circuses to ice shows—and classical ballet.

Studio Height

Another important aspect of a dance studio is its height. Some teachers have been known to operate classes even in the basements of their homes. These low-ceilinged basements are normally designed to take children, but are sometimes used for adults. When jumping across a floor, a person has really more than enough points to keep in mind without the prospect of terrible damage of one kind or another developing from a bump on the head.

Mirrors

Mirrors, mirrors, and more mirrors on the walls are other essential tools that a dancer needs. They should stretch the length of one entire wall at least and be fixed to it. A beginner has to work toward perfecting her alignment and balance, so she must become accustomed to the correct feeling of what that means on her body at the same time training her eye to recognize the look she associates with that feeling. Only by combining the physical with the optical will she develop a complete sense of correct placement. This is good alignment of legs in terms of turnout (hip rotation) and good posture, with all lines coming from the body correctly according to the required position.

The idea of having to develop the correct feeling on the body* as well as the right look is not so ridiculous as it may sound, for the two are very difficult to accomplish. This problem is aggravated if a beginner receives bad training. As the eye is being trained simultaneously with the body, if the student does not learn correct placement, her eye for line will also be distorted. She will eventually be so

---

*No position should be superimposed on any physique. The student should learn to use the leeway that exists, even in classical positions, to suit her own body type. (David Howard)

familiar with seeing herself incorrectly placed that she will become secure with that feeling. If she then moves on to a teacher who tries to correct her placement, it will not feel right on her body, it will not look accurate to her eye, and she is likely to feel very insecure. If she has believed all along she has been working correctly, she may even regard her new teacher with some suspicion, because her judgment will be based on her previous incorrect training.

David Howard talks of this problem of a teacher who is faced not merely with the difficult task of retraining a student physically but also optically. If the student has suffered from really poor training for a number of years, this will also shake up the nervous system, and make her question her chances of becoming a professional. With the grueling day-to-day work and discipline that are required, training the correct way presents enough problems, so to find out one has been working the wrong way, and now has to change one's ideas and method, can be a severe emotional blow and a great setback.

If this seems exaggerated, one has only to take a look at the two great schools from which the Bolshoi and Kirov ballet companies recruit their dancers. They are two of the world's best ballet institutions; only children with long-legged, well-proportioned, and pliable physiques are selected; and the environment offers few distractions, since most of the pupils are boarders. Although they have to maintain high academic standards, and time is allotted to sports and various ballet-related subjects, the priority of each student is to become a ballet dancer of the highest caliber. Hoping to achieve this, the average student must study correctly for eight years. With all this concentrated work, only a small number of the graduates are accepted into the two great companies. Others work with the various lesser ballet companies distributed throughout the Soviet Union, or turn to another form of dance, or maybe teach. A number of students do not even complete the eight years of training.

The Barre

The other important fixture that completes a good studio is the barre. This is a rail of wood or steel in the dance studio which the

The students in *attitude en demi-plié* in a class given by Robert Barnett
at the Atlanta Ballet. This also illustrates one of the several designs
of portable barres. Mr. Barnett is a former member of the New
York City Ballet. *Photo: Jill Fineberg*

dancer holds while doing exercises. Where necessary, portable barres
are also placed in the center of the studio. The barre is significant
from the preballet age of six—at which age a child learns that it is not
to swing on—right on through the training and throughout a professional's career.

The height of the barre should be just above waist level, which, of course, presents problems with growing children. However, many of the best studios that take children have barres at two, or even three, different levels. The purpose of the barre is to permit the student to maintain balance by lightly placing her hand on it, rather than to clutch it for support. Sometimes a teacher will wait until the end of a particular step, when the student should be balanced, then tell her to remove her hand from the barre.

Studio Temperature

Not the least important aspect of the classroom is the temperature. It is not possible for a room to be too hot, and the muscles and joints love it. For that reason many schools are without air conditioning. Where very high temperatures exist for several months of the year, such as in the South or West of the United States, air conditioners are usually installed. However, during the days when the temperature goes up into the nineties or hundreds, it is surprising how much work is accomplished. Warming up at the barre becomes considerably easier, and whole classes find themselves working with a suppleness they did not know they had. Sometimes fans are used in studios but these simply circulate the stale air rather than cool it.

One point for the student to guard against when working in excessively hot weather, with or without air conditioning, is a false sense of being warmed up. The body always needs to be warmed up slowly and thoroughly, and the feeling of being too hot does not mean the muscles are automatically ready for the strenuous activity demanded by ballet.* An improperly warmed body is inevitably more prone to injury, and the only advantage of excessive heat is that the body will be more pliable, somewhat reducing the risk of injury as the dancer works. In fact, one problem faced by dancers in harsh winters is that they almost never feel properly warm.

Very hot weather also precludes the necessity for extra layers of

*See "Barre Exercises," page 24.

clothing,* with the exception of leg warmers, and students who suc-
cumb to wearing these layers are most likely to be wearing them as a
security blanket. It is actually inadvisable to wear unnecessary layers
of clothing in excessive heat, since the body's natural thermostat becomes greatly overworked at keeping the inside temperature normal.
Since the work done in a good ballet class causes most people to per-
spire excessively, it is unreasonable to put further demands on the
body. Overheating can cause dizziness and, in extreme cases, even
fainting.

David Howard talks of the problems he is faced with when working in air conditioning, because it counteracts all the hard work that is
being done to warm the muscles. "Sometimes you look around after a
very healthy barre, thinking the results are going to be marvelous,
until you realize they're all frozen stiff. It looks as if they haven't
done any work at all—most unrewarding."

Heat also speeds up a class in that it is not really possible to start
correcting body placement and movement until the students are
warm and their bodies pliable. One day, when Mr. Howard was told
it was 103 degrees, his reply was, "Maybe it's a little bit warm, no
oxygen in the air, and it's not much fun when you can't breathe."

To a dancer, such concerns as breathing are secondary (even if she
is constantly running to the water fountain). Having a body warm
enough to work with is of paramount importance, and this is one reason a ballet class is begun with barre exercises.

As dancers thrive on heat, studios are usually kept at a temperature otherwise uncomfortable even in the winter. The students push,
they sweat, they pant—but their bodies flourish and work the better
for it.

TEACHER'S PERSONAL APPEARANCE

A teacher's personal appearance can sometimes be deceptive, and
can not always be expected to be a correct indication as to whether or
not her teaching will be up to standard. A teacher once brought

*See "Dress," pages 41–44.

Lupe Serrano, former principal with American Ballet Theatre, teaching class at the School of the Pennsylvania Ballet. She is demonstrating *attitude devant. Photo: Ken Duncan*

twelve girls from Ohio to audition for David Howard in New York City. This woman turned up in a silver mink, dripping with diamonds, and displaying long fingernails. She then casually informed Mr. Howard that "they can do anything you want them to, honey! They can kick, split, spin, and leap," making them sound like a circus act that had turned up at the wrong audition. At that point, Mr. Howard was requested to put them through their paces, though he felt extremely skeptical about the students' potential.

Twelve well-groomed girls came into the room and produced astounding results. They were given a very difficult class and not only could they "kick, split, spin, and leap," but they could do it all so competently that eleven of them were offered scholarships. "If you think they're good, honey," continued the teacher, "I've got plenty more back where they came from who are even better."

Such a glamorous theatrical look is not normally associated with serious ballet teachers who, during teaching sessions, will usually be simply dressed. The women will wear ballet clothes, possibly adding a wide, loosely fitting skirt, and the men will often be in pants made of a material that will give, and a tee shirt. Usually teachers need to be dressed in clothes that give them the freedom to demonstrate the steps they want to be carried out, even to those students who are quite advanced. On occasion, a teacher will show a class the right way and the wrong way to do a certain movement, as injury can so easily result from doing a step incorrectly. Mme Gabriela Darvash, who has her own ballet school in New York, experienced an unpleasant back injury when demonstrating how *not* to do a cabriole.* She pulled a muscle when landing badly, and the class learned an unfortunate lesson. Anyone who has seen a teacher injure herself in such a demonstration cannot fail to appreciate the importance of working correctly.

*"A movement in the air, in which the legs are at an angle to the floor and the lower leg beats against the upper leg." *The Dance Encyclopedia*, rev. and enl. Compiled and edited by Anatole Chujoy and P. W. Manchester (New York: Simon & Schuster, 1967).

Dancers in David Howard's class in first arabesque, *relevé* (on the ball of the foot), with high arm. *Photo: Steven Caras*

Teachers who have danced for many years will usually hold themselves very erect as they move around the studio. They will be possessed of both gracefulness and the characteristic walk, in which the feet are turned out more than the average person's, due to the turnout that will have been developed in the hip sockets, if it was not a gift of nature to begin with.

Patricia Wilde demonstrates second arabesque (of four) to students in the scholarship class at the American Ballet Theatre School.
Photo: Steven Caras

Teachers and Teaching

A TEACHER'S CREDENTIALS

The credentials of a teacher should also be examined carefully. Just because an instructor is a member of a Teachers' Convention,* does not mean that she will be competent. Although many of these teachers do have a great deal of knowledge, others show an alarming lack of it.

Any teacher qualified through the examinations of the Royal Academy of Dancing† (a British organization) will most probably be reliable. Also, those that have been trained by any of the top company schools could be expected to be proficient, especially if they have spent some time dancing with those same companies. However, this is by no means a reliable recommendation on its own and each class should be examined carefully in all areas.

CLASSES

Preballet Training

The length and organization of a class are aspects that will vary according to the ages and levels of the students and the convictions of a teacher. Ballet training should not be given to children under the

---

* One of the teachers' organizations that hold annual formal assemblies of their members for discussion and action on matters of common concern.

† See R.A.D. statement of purpose, pages 35–36.

age of eight, as the body is not sufficiently developed to be able to take the strain, and healthy, natural growth will be hampered. Pre-ballet instruction can safely be given to a child of six or seven, as it does not impair development, and some brave teachers even take on classes of four- and five-year-olds. Barbara Thuesen took on such a class, where the little four-year-old girls all became jelly beans, according to the color of their leotards. She spent most of her time teaching them to understand music and how to tell right from left.

Even at the ages of six and seven, a child should be doing only the simplest things related to ballet. It is not worth pushing a child, especially at so young an age, but if she is introduced to a class and then wants to join in, the child could well enjoy it a great deal. Certainly a group of these tinies can be enchanting to watch. One minute they will have earnest expressions on their faces as they try to work something out for themselves, and the next they will be watching their teacher as she explains and demonstrates, their eyes wide, standing with swaybacks and tummies sticking out, as they become absorbed in what she is doing.

What should be emphasized is that a child at this stage must not start ballet exercises. She should be taught to listen to music and shown simply how to move to it, so that she will develop a sense of the way music and movement go together. At the American Ballet Center* one of the great favorites is to walk around the room to the call of "icicle, icicle; marshmallow, marshmallow," which is walking on *demi-pointe*, with the legs straight, straight; *plié, plié.*

The parts of the body can be taught. Even a young child will usually know where her knee is, because she probably skins it frequently, but at that age she can learn where her stomach is and that it should not stick out, and to stand up straight and sit correctly so her posture will develop well. By the time she starts ballet, she should know where her ankles, thighs, and hips are, and for her ear to be tuned to some of the easy French terminology† will be to her advantage, though it is not essential.

* Official school of the Joffrey Ballet Company.
† See "How Familiar Is the Teacher with French Terminology?" pages 59–61.

Two preballet students at the School of Cleveland Ballet
discovering *port de bras* and sitting in frog position, so that the
turnout will not be forced. The arms are in fifth position *en haut*
(above), and the position of the legs is a literal translation from
the French *grenouille* (frog).

In this way, a young child's eyes and ears are being trained and, if she is taught to mimic, it will help her toward picking up combinations later on. When a dancer works with a competent teacher, especially one who is also a choreographer, the combinations of steps given in class are sometimes very complex and therefore, the sooner a child learns to follow instructions, the better.

At this stage, a young child is capable of seeing an angle look different from a curved line. For example, bending the elbow produces an angle, whereas the two arms held outward with the fingertips almost touching, and the elbows very slightly bent, results in a somewhat imperfect circle. In ballet, where the arms are always soft, a dancer needs to know the difference and a young child can benefit from early eye training.

A child of this age can also learn to "spot" her head, which is the special way a dancer has of moving it when doing turns, so as to avoid becoming dizzy. She will keep her eyes focused on a particular point in front of her (which, when learning, will be her own reflection in the mirror), until the last possible moment, and then focus back again as soon as possible. Some may have a hard time focusing, while others may focus and not register what they see. Both these points are important to develop, in order to prevent dizziness and ensuing calamity. This usually takes a long time to work on and at the preballet stage a child can begin with a type of *chaîné**—two half turns to complete the full circle—to give the feeling of how the head works.

Even at this young age, there should be discipline in a class because then it will not come as such a shock for the eight-year-old who begins ballet. As Meredith Baylis, teacher at American Ballet Center, explained: "They should not be allowed to run around playing butterflies and being cute. They should have their little steps to do." However, it is not possible to force a child to take ballet seriously and if she does not develop an interest, she is probably in the wrong place.

---

* *Chaîné*, chain, link. In the plural, abbreviation of the term *tours chaînés déboulés*: a series of rapid turns on *pointes* or *demi-pointes* done in a straight line or a circle.

Beginning Ballet

Then comes the time that a child reaches the age of eight and is ready for the first ballet class. When thinking in terms of classical ballet, it is important to remember that the way the training is given actually dictates whether or not it is a ballet class. Many schools are

Young students at the School of the Minnesota Dance Theatre learning feeling in the hips as they place the right leg in *tendu en arrière. Photo: Joseph Ketola*

designed just for "fun, fun, fun" and to bring in the dollars. These should *not* be considered ballet classes.

A story once reached David Howard of a student who, after seeing a production of *Swan Lake* on public television by one of the world's leading companies, approached her teacher somewhat dismayed, because she had never done anything the likes of which she had seen on that program. The girl was a young teenager, and when

A group of young students in class at the School of the Pennsylvania Ballet. *Photo: Mildred Keil*

she questioned her training with her teacher, the answer was, quite simply, "Well, dear, you're not ready for that real ballet yet." This is a common excuse heard from teachers caught in such a situation.

Even for a child who is taking "real" ballet, being ready is a state that almost never exists in the vocabulary of ballet performances, from the time a student does her first concert to the day she ends her professional career. More often than not a dancer, or maybe a ballet master, will suffer from premier nerves and the feeling that the performance will not be quite up to par for lack of rehearsal time. This is one of the very important aspects where good training will show through on all levels—even a young child's first concert. If she is well taught up to the level to be expected of her in that performance, then, somehow, she will be able to handle it. She may even make mistakes, but she will have the ability to work around them.

Length of Classes

At the preballet stage, a class should not be longer than half an hour. Between the ages of eight and ten, a child's attention span is usually still very short and she will probably only be able to work constructively in a class that is from forty-five minutes to an hour long. From the age of eleven to fourteen, one and a quarter to one and a half hours is an appropriate length of time. This is also the age range where a girl's concentration is likely to waver almost more than any other, because this is the time she will probably reach puberty and her life will be full of profundity. She will start to be aware of boys, who will possibly dominate her life, and the idea of struggling through a ballet class, when she could be reveling in her romantic dreams either of the boy next door or of her favorite movie hero, will probably not appeal to her. However, if she is the kind of girl more prone to dreaming about Mikhail Baryshnikov or Peter Martins, she is more likely to participate with enthusiasm.

Although this is a phase to watch out for, it is not any great cause for alarm. If a child is serious about ballet, by the age of fifteen or sixteen she should start to settle down. By this time she should be taking a two-hour class, which is the length of many professional-level classes, although a few teachers are known to go for as long as two and a half hours. This can happen when the classes are very large and the students full of energy. To begin with, it will take extra time to put a large class through all the combinations done in the center of the floor. For this, the dancers will be divided into small groups which will vary according to the size of the studio. For high, open jumps, there may even be as few as three to six of them moving across the floor at once. In an advanced, or professional, class that may contain as many as sixty or eighty anxious workers, this will add a fair amount of time.*

Barre Exercises

Through barre exercises, the entire body is warmed up, slowly and thoroughly, and for this reason many of the best schools spend from thirty-five to forty-five minutes in this pursuit, in classes that vary from one and a half to two and a half hours at the intermediate and advanced stages.

The parent of a student at David Howard's school provided a good example of lack of knowledge of the ballet class. Having watched her daughter's first class, the mother approached Mr. Howard and informed him, "She already knows those barre exercises, you don't have to worry with them anymore."

Barre exercises are a very arduous part of ballet training, but even though they may be monotonous, they are a fundamental necessity. One of the hardest rules to learn in ballet is that the person who tries to dance before her body is sufficiently warm is going to shorten her career considerably. As witness to that fact is one of the world's great male dancers, Rudolf Nureyev. Now over forty years old, Mr. Nureyev still takes class daily, even when he is not performing. Such days are few and far between since he still does about two hundred performances a year. It is unlikely that he would have been able to maintain such a feat without his outstanding discipline and capacity for hard work. As David Howard remarked, "What one tries to produce is a

---

* Outside New York, where classes are usually smaller, many at the professional level last only an hour and a half.

body that will stand the test of time. That is most important."

During the mornings, especially, a teacher will usually give a long, slow barre because, since a dancer will be working on her placement as well as warming up, it is important for her to work on her body slowly.

Children at the School of Cleveland Ballet doing barre exercises. They are in *tendu devant* with the arms in third position. Here the barres are on two levels. (Other photos show two or three levels.)

On the day of Ivan Nagy's final retirement gala, company class was held at noon. The dancers were all very tired, as the stage at the Kennedy Center in Washington, D.C., is extremely rough on the anatomy, and the American Ballet Theatre had already been dancing there for two weeks. One of the ballet masters, Michael Lland, eased the company through slow pliés, as each dancer worked on her sore muscles and aching joints, maybe inclining her head as she watched herself in the mirror, with an expression that said it was particularly tough that afternoon. Several observers were present on that occasion, including one familiar with the New York City Ballet, a company renowned for its speed. Finding it all very amusing, she remarked, "Oh, what a lovely slow pace; I wish I could have taken such classes. A City Ballet class would have been over by now." The company had been working for just ten minutes.

This was only the observer's lighthearted way of referring to the fact that the New York City Ballet is known to work at a fast pace in class because it is a company that must move fast onstage. Quite often Mr. Balanchine will start his classes with a barre that lasts only ten minutes. However, the reason for this is that he expects his dancers to come in early and warm themselves up at the barre before he arrives.

Class Organization

The way a class should be divided up in terms of barre and center work depends entirely on the individual teacher, his school of thought, and the purpose of the class.

As a standard class, Andrei Kramarevsky, with the School of American Ballet, would like to see a combination of Russian and American training as, he says, both have their strong features. He mentioned that a company class in the Soviet Union is one hour long, with the time divided equally between the barre and the work done

---

Older students at the School of Cleveland Ballet in *attitude en demi-plié,* instructed by Dennis Nahat.

in the center. In the Russian ballet schools, the barre takes thirty minutes out of a one and a half-hour class, and the last half-hour is devoted to working on the jump. The reason the Russians tend to have
a longer jump, he says, is that the preparation is better, so that the
body, head, and arms go together with the feet, making the jump
longer. In the United States, the jump is held back by the rest of the
body not taking off as fast as the feet. However, he admires the extra
time given to barre work in this country, as this does give strength to
the legs and feet.

There are occasions when a class structure will vary, such as
when the girls are beginning pointe* work, and the teacher needs to
pay special attention to each individual. This is the time when boys
can put extra concentration and work into their double tours,† and
the teacher will need to devote some time to each one of them.

Some teachers include exercises in their classes that are carried
out lying on the floor. These give a very clear sense of alignment, and
a class may be divided into half an hour of floor exercises, half an
hour at the barre, and the final thirty minutes on the feet away from
the barre.

During the course of a good class, a student learns how to work
with her own body. It is a process of discovering the weaknesses and
strengths and what needs to be put right. A dancer will find out what
patterns of movement she finds difficult and can work on ironing out
those problems, rather than waiting to discover what they are only
when working with a choreographer.

A teacher to avoid is the one who gives twenty minutes of ballet,
twenty minutes of tap, and maybe even twenty minutes of jazz in a
one-hour class. This often happens in the commercial schools. David
Howard talks of the confusion to students and does not think that
the right mood can be developed for each individual requirement.
Somehow the feeling will be wrong if the child has to keep changing

---

* The toe. The position of the foot in which there is a continuous straight line from the toe
on which the dancer stands, through the instep, ankle, knee, and hip. . . . In ballet, only women
dance on pointe. From *The Dance Encyclopedia*.

† *Tour*—in ballet, a turn. A double tour is two turns in the air—(*double tour en l'air*). (David
Howard)

from one type of dance to another—and this presents its difficulties. By the time the appropriate mood is established, it is time to move on again. Also, it is difficult to combine ballet with jazz or tap because they are not really related. They are separate art forms, and therefore it is difficult to switch from one to the other. Most important of all, it is certainly not possible to accomplish anything in ballet with the occasional twenty-minute class.

If a child does want to study other forms of dance, it will be to

Students from the Stone Camryn School of Ballet performing a Polish folk dance.

her advantage as long as she takes them as separate classes. If she intends to become a professional ballet dancer it is actually advisable
that she study some modern dance and jazz. Even the established
classical ballet companies now include in their repertoire ballets that
are at least contemporary, if not strictly modern, as well as those requiring jazz movements. It is not a good idea for a child's training to
be so rigidly classical that she eventually finds it difficult to move in
any other style. The problem is that then not only does a dancer have
a hard time feeling comfortable with other styles, she sometimes also
looks quite wrong in a certain role.

The technique of the character dance is also very important. Not
found in the classic dance, this is a special technique in ballet involving different muscles. Once a dancer becomes proficient in this, she
becomes master of the character dances of the various nationalities,
such as Russian, Hungarian, Spanish, etc. It is a common misconcep-
tion to think of the character dance simply as the study of folk
dances of different nationalities.

Frequency of Classes

The question as to how often a child should take class depends
very much on her enthusiasm. Those who succeed as dancers often
become quite serious about ballet when they are very young, and are
taking daily classes by the age of nine, although this is not necessary.
David Howard feels a young child can take class once or twice a
week, but by the time she reaches the age of twelve she should be
studying five or six times a week, if she develops a strong interest.
The point is, the more a child takes class, the better.

Style of Teaching/Syllabus

Although a person walking into a class for the first time would
probably not be able to recognize one style from another, it is at least
important that she know what these styles are and to what extent
they are taught in this country.

The *Russian* school was developed from the old Italian and French

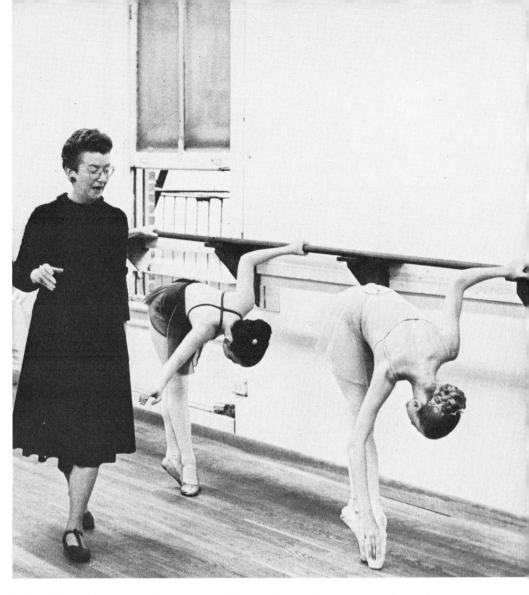

Mme Darvash instructing some of her advanced young students in *penché en avant en sous-sus*. *Photo: Steven Caras*

schools and, having taken the best from these, the Russians added their own genius and ethnic stamp over the years. They place a great deal of emphasis on *épaulement*,* carriage, *port de bras*,† and expression.

* "The use of the shoulders in presenting a step to the audience." From *The Dance Encyclopedia*.

† Movement of the arms.

They also believe very strongly in a balanced training; that it is as important to be able to do steps as deftly to the right as to the left. An outstanding characteristic of the beautiful Russian style is that it rarely presents its dancers squarely facing the audience. After the Russian Revolution in 1917, the style was spread outside the Soviet Union, mainly to Europe and the United States, by the Ballet Russe de Monte Carlo, under successive directors, Serge Diaghilev, René Blum, and Colonel W. de Basil, and finally Sergei Denham. Many illustrious members of this company (which ceased performing in 1963), as well as others, have helped maintain the Russian school through teaching. There are no examinations.

The *Soviet* system of ballet education has its roots in the Russian school, but has added new and higher developments, based on the principles founded by Agrippina Vaganova.* They are hallmarked by the broad and sweeping movements of the Russian school, combined with a strong and buoyant technique. There is always great emphasis on the music and pupils are taught to dance music, instead of to dance *to* music, so that it is in their blood from a very early age. Music dominates the Soviet style of dancing and its choreography. There are no examinations in the Soviet system of ballet education, though it usually takes eight years to master, as mentioned earlier.†

Despite the fact that the Russian/Soviet styles are characterized by their broad and sweeping movements, Patricia Wilde, Director of American Ballet Theatre School, states: "The training should be simple. If it becomes too flamboyant, uncontrolled, and full of mannerisms, that is a sign of bad Russian training."

Cecchetti. This style is named after Enrico Cecchetti, himself a great dancer, who first became recognized as a great teacher when he became second Ballet Master of the Imperial Theatre in St. Petersburg, Russia, in 1890. In his hands, many Russian dancers of the time made brilliant technical progress, such as had not been known there before that time. The Cecchetti technique specifically displays outstanding footwork and the dancers are known also for their strength.

Appropriately, the "Blue Bird" in *The Sleeping Beauty* was choreo-

---

* Agrippina Vaganova (1879–1951). Great Russian ballerina and one of the greatest masters of ballet of all time.

† See page 9.

graphed on Enrico Cecchetti. It includes a variation,* followed by a coda† which contains a series of *brisés volés*,†† requiring brilliant footwork and great strength. In fact, this piece of choreography is acknowledged as the hardest for a man in all of the classical ballet repertoire.

Cecchetti developed a specific syllabus and there is a series of examinations by which a student's progress is evaluated.

Talking of the Cecchetti method, Patricia Wilde spoke of the developments: "A sign of poor Cecchetti training is that it is too closed in. Nowadays the style is much more open."

R.A.D. The Royal Academy of Dancing is a nonprofit organization, originally established in England to promote the teaching of classical ballet and national dances, which puts great emphasis on the *correct* teaching of classical ballet. The teaching draws on various other syllabuses, and there is a three-year required teachers' training course which must be taken, and certification received before a person can give instruction. As well as ballet, the course includes subjects such as dance history, character, music, French, mime, and related sciences— anatomy and biology. There are also student examinations, and the school encourages dance as a part of education, whether or not a student intends to become a professional.

The following statement puts the purposes very well:

THE ROYAL ACADEMY OF DANCING

UNITED STATES OF AMERICA

"The Royal Academy"
by the President—Dame Margot Fonteyn de Arias, D.B.E., D. Mus.

The Royal Academy of Dancing is, I believe, the only organization of its kind in the world that pays serious attention to the

* The second part of a classic *pas de deux*, following the *adagio* (combination of steps done to slow music).

† The third part of the classic pas de deux, which follows the variations.... also the finale of a classic ballet in which all principals appear separately or with their partners. From *The Dance Encyclopedia*.

†† A flying *brisé* (which is, literally, a broken movement). Basically, a series of jumps requiring very difficult and complex movements of the legs and feet.

young children who are *never* going to be ballet dancers, but who nevertheless study ballet dancing.

Obviously the majority of young children in any dancing class will not want to make a career in ballet when they grow up. Most of them would be quite unsuited to it anyway.

The Royal Academy of Dancing believes that it is very frustrating for a child to be working at something which she has no possibility of ever being able to master. A serious ballet training is far too difficult, and physically beyond the capability of the average child. To take such a training can only lead to heartbreak and a sense of frustration; but no matter what career a child may eventually follow, there is very much in dancing in its highest form (which is what I believe ballet to be) that can help her.

The Academy regards the art of ballet as a valuable part of general education. Our *syllabus for children's examinations* has been worked out in close *cooperation* with *the English educational authorities.* It is taught once a week in many general schools as part of their curriculum.

School teachers welcome this work because the children acquire a sense of coordination and of discipline which are a great asset, particularly for sports and athletics.

The national and character dances in the syllabus fulfill the natural instinct of all peoples to enjoy their folk dances, and bring the children into realistic contact with the root folklore of other nations.

The mime and free expression provide training and development for each child's imagination and dramatic instincts.

Above all, the basic ballet work not only instills an appreciation of the art but it is the best foundation for those children who are in fact talented and will progress to a full, serious ballet training from ten or eleven years old, which is the best age to start. The Academy has a quite separate syllabus for the serious students. The first examination in this series can be taken at the age of thirteen.

Early training with a bad teacher can undoubtedly ruin the possibility of a successful career in ballet. *Parents* all over the world welcome the *reassurance* that their child is in good safe hands with a teacher who bases her work on the R.A.D. syllabus.

The *teachers* themselves welcome the *reassurance* that is brought by our examiners, who travel all over the world, that their teaching is up to a certain high standard. But some people may ask what is the point of children entering examinations at all. To my mind, the most important point is the sense of achievement, plus a pride and satisfaction in the mastery of their own limbs. They also learn to understand and respect the art of ballet and feel an added confidence in themselves because they are learning to move with grace and coordination.

I believe that my serious approach to my work was engendered in the respect I felt for the R.A.D. certificates I had made such efforts to gain as a very young child. They were framed and hung on my wall, a source of great comfort in the long forgotten tribulations of childhood.

The Royal Academy of Dancing is not a school, it has no pupils. It works in cooperation but has no actual connection with the Royal Ballet Company. It is a non-profit-making organization devoted solely to raising teaching standards and helping to give children as much as possible of genuine and lasting value through the art of dancing.

Bournonville. This is the style named after August Bournonville (1805–1879), Danish choreographer and teacher. Bournonville developed a series of exercises for each day of the week, Monday through Saturday, as Cecchetti did after him. To this day these exercises are used as the basis for the training at the Royal Danish Ballet, although now other major influences have been absorbed.

As shown by the Royal Danish Ballet, Bournonville-trained men exude strength and vigor, and display outstanding elevation and *batterie,** while the women radiate femininity. They are altogether a very impressive reflection of the Romantic period, and execute their steps with an exceptionally light and airy quality. The use of mime

* "A generic term applied to all movements in which the feet beat together or one foot beats against the other." From *The Dance Encyclopedia.*

and character dances in ballet is also a great Bournonville hallmark.

It is interesting to note that Bournonville and Cecchetti were both experts in the respective features for which their styles have become famous, and it is thanks to their own brilliant understanding of the technique needed to develop these characteristics that enabled them to pass on their skills to future generations.

Enrico Cecchetti was a great admirer of August Bournonville, although he did not agree with him on all points, and was familiar with the *Études Choréographique*, written by the latter. Cecchetti wrote the *Manuel des Exercises de Danse Théâtrale à Pratiquer Chaque Jour de la Semaine, à l'usage de mes élèves*.* Apparently the two men knew each other, though Cecchetti was much younger and wrote his work fifteen years after the death of Bournonville.

Since the purpose of this book is to help an individual recognize a good ballet class, it is worth quoting Messrs. Bournonville and Cecchetti.†

"Exercises at the barre," said August Bournonville, "are only necessary to prepare one without too much fatigue for the lesson itself. Forced methods for turning out the feet and hips are, in my opinion, far from being good, but are ugly, ridiculous, offensive and almost entirely useless."

Then Cecchetti wrote: "It is evident that a dancer should surmount and conquer all obstacles which his physique places in the way of his dancing; but it is not by taking one foot in his hand and torturing it in order to turn it out, nor in putting one foot on the barre in order to raise it high and split oneself; but it is in sober exercises that one succeeds in conquering obstacles. To force†† the legs, for one should indeed render them obedient to the requirements of the theory, one holds to the barre . . .

"Once one is master of the legs, one proceeds to the center to acquire equilibrium, then on demi-pointe to acquire steady balance.

* [Manual of exercises of theatrical dance, to be practiced each day of the week, for the use of my pupils].

† All quotes from Bournonville and Cecchetti are taken from *Bournonville and Ballet Technique*, by Erik Bruhn and Lillian Moore. (New York: Macmillan & Co., 1961, republished by *Dance Horizons*).

†† Although not literally. The word here means force in the sense of train.

Once sure of balance and equilibrium one proceeds to *temps d'adagio.*"*
He then goes on to explain how positions are perfected and strength
and endurance acquired in adagio. Only then, he says, should one begin the *temps d'allegro*† (jumps, turns, beats, etc.).

The accepted American style is unique to the New York City Ballet, having been developed by George Balanchine. Not only has he
developed this style, which has been termed neo-classical, but its
very essence takes his continuous presence to maintain. With regard
to teaching styles in the United States, the term American applies
rather to the many different methods used by the various teachers
who glean what they consider to be the best of the established
schools and add their own theories, from which they develop their
own uniqueness.

Although the styles in which classes are taught vary and are a
point to be taken into consideration, there is no syllabus which companies look for in preference to any other, unless the director of a
particular company happens to be a strong believer in a certain
school. As Ms. Wilde says: "What the companies want is quite simply well-trained classical dancers."

Bournonville is the only style mentioned here that is not widely
taught in the United States. It is taught in Denmark, and Ballet West
Summer Course offers classes in this technique. The reason it is mentioned here is its significance as a classical form.

Although it is all right to study with more than one teacher, Ms.
Wilde emphasizes the importance of a child staying with one style
when young. Preferably, a child who is working toward being accepted by a dance company should enter the appropriate school (if there
is one, as with all the major companies) by the age of fourteen or fifteen. In the case of those company schools that offer scholarships, the
competition is very tough. Talking of a recent scholarship audition of
thirteen- to seventeen-year-olds at American Ballet Theatre School,
Ms. Wilde said that of the 280 who applied, six were accepted. During another audition held in California, three were taken from the

* In this sense, a series of exercises during a ballet lesson designed to develop grace, a sense
of line, and balance, and done to slow music.

† In a class, part of the lesson that follows the adagio, done to a fast or moderate tempo.

two hundred who applied. Girls will have greater numbers to compete against than boys—at least for the foreseeable future.

Ms. Wilde, who has toured schools extensively for the Ford Foundation, said she is pleased to see nowadays that teachers are becoming more and more aware that they cannot simply teach a routine, that they do have to understand the reasons for the steps and combinations they are teaching.

Any of the strictly classical styles will always provide a solid foundation from which to adapt later on. Scott Barnard, Ballet Master with the Joffrey Ballet, is always happy to see Cecchetti-trained dancers come into the company, since he feels it gives such pure classical training from which a dancer can develop.

While David Howard is a supporter of the various different syllabuses, believing in the excellence of the training, he feels they can be limiting, because then a dancer spends so much time learning a syllabus she becomes more proficient at dealing with that than learning how to dance—flow of movement being so important.

Number of Students per Class

The size of a class a child is entering is extremely important. At the preballet stage, a group of eight to ten is a good number. Up to the age of ten there could be as many as twelve in a class and there certainly should not be more than fifteen. Children need to be constantly reminded of the basic points, such as pulling up out of the hips and keeping their stomachs in. Such things are often forgotten, as all energy and concentration are put into learning steps, and perfection of line needs to be watched over to make a child sufficiently aware of the importance of training the eye as well as the body.

Although a professional class can work with as many as twenty or thirty dancers, anything more than that number is basically not a good idea, and even though most of the top teachers are obliged to work with greater numbers, it really does become a great strain for them. Apart from the time wasted by the students in standing around waiting their turn to do the steps, it becomes harder for the teacher to give specific corrections. Although an advanced student should be aware as to whether or not a particular remark applies to her, she may not know that she is not doing a particular step correctly. Sometimes she is unaware of just where she is going wrong, and only a teacher who appreciates the misunderstanding will be capable of putting that dancer right. If a class is very large, as it is with some open classes, a teacher may keep missing the fact that a dancer is repeatedly making the same mistake. This reduces the chance that the student will ever learn it correctly.

Frank Bourman demonstrates *tendu en arrière* to children at the School of the Minnesota Dance Theatre. *Photo: Joseph Ketola*

One serious problem that stems from this is that a dancer begins to believe she is properly positioned. A repeated mistake starts to feel correct. As Mme Darvash explains, "Some of them may have the best training but they don't understand what's right on their bodies. One can never give a correction and expect each individual to know how to apply it to herself. Each of them has to be given the necessary personal attention."

This is something that applies even to a professional dancer and throughout her career she will need guidance. Sometimes she may even reach a point where she feels stuck in her technique, and in the words of one well-known New York teacher, "A teacher must have a way of working that has growth. A dancer is only as good as the teacher she is working with, so if the teacher's theories get stuck, then the dancer gets stuck." This particular teacher herself suffered from bad training in her childhood. After experiencing the damage that could be done emotionally and physically, she decided to develop her own way of teaching. Now, she is one of the most respected teachers of ballet in New York City.

Dress and Footwear

DRESS

Pupils' clothing also can be a good indication of general classroom standards. They should be dressed in leotards, tights, and ballet slippers, and girls should have their hair neatly tied back if it is long and avoid wearing nail polish. Although some students may wish to wear brightly colored clothes, it is not very advisable. Black leotards and pink tights may seem ordinary but there is a practical reason for them. It is important for a teacher to see the muscles on a student's legs and pink tights allow for this. Also, it is less tiring on the eye to be looking at a group of people similarly dressed. Consequently, the student who dresses appropriately shows herself to have the more professional approach. Some schools actually establish the color of the clothing to be worn in their classes. Leotards are made in a variety of styles and produced in both nylon and cotton. For those who feel that pink and black are too much like a dancer's uniform, when given the choice, there are several other similar colors available. An extra item that will be needed by the boys is the dance-belt. This is a strong supporter worn under the tights.

Preballet students should have bare legs and be dressed only in leotards, socks, and ballet slippers. This enables the teacher to see the leg muscles most clearly, which is necessary at this stage.

Extra clothing is also an item to watch carefully. Muscles must be warm to be able to work properly, and to be able to perform the feats required of them without causing injury. To help achieve this warmth more quickly, the use of leg warmers is a good idea as they will cause the dancer to retain more body heat and facilitate execution of the barre exercises. This is a very positive way to benefit the overworked legs from which every dancer suffers. Leg warmers are among the most prevalent and valued articles of clothing for any dancer, and they were invented by Alexandra Danilova during the days she danced for the Ballet Russe de Monte Carlo. Mme Danilova must have suffered more than most from cold limbs, having taken class in the bitter temperatures of the Russian winter, during the days

These students at the School of Cleveland Ballet are in *arabesque face à la barre,* making use of the two barre levels. Note the neatness of young students here and in the other photographs. There is an absence of extra clothing, and it is only among the older students that added layers will be noticed.

after the Russian Revolution when she was dancing at the Maryinsky Theatre in Leningrad and the ballet studios were not even heated.

When warming the muscles, however, it is extremely important to make sure that they can breathe. That is to say they have to be able to absorb the air around them, which means that as they sweat freely, they should be coated in a material that can absorb the sweat. Judging from ballet studios, even in the most illustrious companies, this appears to be the era of plastic pants. They are sometimes worn as brief as shorts, rolled up to the groin. They are worn knee-length, they are worn full-length, sometimes fixed in such a way that they seal off all entrances and exits for air from the waist to the ankles. Now they are even being produced to cover the entire body. As the muscles are worked, they sweat, and they then suffer from lack of air circulation and an absorbent coating. This results in the moisture being trapped around the body and in time the muscles actually become weakened.

Often dancers will claim to wear plastic pants in order to lose weight, and sometimes they may simply be going through an uncertain period, and be wearing them quite literally as a security blanket to cover up because they feel "fat." With occasional exceptions—the professional dancer's idea of being fat probably means that she has put on three pounds. To the casual observer it would probably be unnoticeable—but she perceives herself as suddenly having a big stomach or fat thighs. When it is considered that it is not uncommon for a dancer of five feet seven to weigh 105 pounds, it is easy to see that an extra pound in the wrong place might be obvious to her. The weight-loss theory is actually incorrect. All the plastic pants cause is excessive loss of water and some salt through perspiration, and the body simply becomes dehydrated. Most good teachers do not approve of plastic pants, since they hide the line of the body and this is essential if correct instruction is to be given. At the School of American Ballet,* American Ballet Theatre School, and the American Ballet Center, they are forbidden. As Basil Thompson, who teaches at the latter school, remarked, "With those pants all the heat is kept in and once

---

* Official school of the New York City Ballet.

you take them off, it's like going into ice water, which immediately makes the muscles contract and doesn't do any good at all."

If dancers need to wear an extra layer over leg warmers, then fabric sweat pants are ideal. They are even to be recommended if a dancer is standing around in the middle of a rehearsal, or during filming. In a rehearsal of Glen Tetley's ballet *Contredances*, Anthony Dowell put on sweat pants, plus a sweater over his shoulders, while standing aside for ten minutes as Natalia Makarova rehearsed her variation. The sweat pants were worn over both leg and ankle warmers, which he wore throughout the ninety-minute rehearsal. The month was September, the place New York City, and the temperature in the seventies. Even though he had danced the taxing role of Siegfried in *Swan Lake* the night before with American Ballet Theatre at the Metropolitan Opera House, Mr. Dowell was simply taking the normal precautions that would be taken by most professional dancers.

FOOTWEAR

Careful attention should be given to the feet from the beginning, since this part of the body will have to take a great deal of abuse. In the old days, in China, once a lady had been used to having her feet bound, it was said that she suffered the most excruciating pain if the bonds were ever removed. However, the treatment that some dancers give their feet seems little better, especially once they are wearing pointe shoes and must start to build up calluses on their toes, purely against the punishment their feet will have to take over the years.

Some manufacturers of shoes which are available in this country are Capezio, Frederick Freed of London, Gamba, and Selva.* The first two are the principal suppliers of the companies and also distribute widely among students of ballet.

The size of a dancer's ballet slippers and pointe shoes will not be the same as street shoes, since the grading is not comparable, and this

* Their addresses can be found at the end of this book, pages 126–27.

applies to both domestic and foreign manufacturers. Feet should be measured at the store before shoes are bought. Slippers are made in leather or canvas. Canvas are preferred by many because they shrink back to size after being worn. They are also cheaper than leather. They should fit firmly so that they do not move around, and fit snugly at the heels, though should never be too tight at the toes. On occasion, a dancer will buy a pair of shoes that fits correctly and then, in hot weather, her feet may swell before she puts them on. If they need to be stretched, shoes can be wetted and then stuffed *very* tightly with paper and either left to dry naturally, put on a radiator, or in a warm oven. This should be kept at minimum temperature, since the idea is to dry them out—not roast them. This tactic is also used, minus the stuffing, to dry out shoes after they have become wet from use. Dancers also sometimes wet their shoes while they are wearing them. It is a common sight around dance studios to see girls standing with a foot in the water fountain. This prevents the shoe from sliding around.

Pointe shoes are made of satin, and have a leather sole lined with special material which is the shank. The box at the toe is made of buckram, felt, and a special paste (the secret ingredients of which are carefully guarded by the manufacturers). It is extremely important the box be properly fitted to the toes. It should hold them snugly but not be so tight that the toes are bunched together. The vamp (or part of the box that covers the top of the foot) should be long enough to cover the joint at the base of the big toe. If a girl has a high arch, it should be slightly longer, since she will need the support. A vamp the same length as the toes will not support the dancer when she is on pointe. Correct fitting of pointe shoes cannot be overemphasized, since without this, permanent damage can be done to the feet, and the risk of injury when dancing is heightened.

Capezio has several types of shoes under the names of Pavlova, Nicolini, Assoluta, Contempora, and Ultimo. The first three are tapered shoes of different weights, ranging from Pavlova—the hardest toe—to Assoluta—the lightest. Contempora has the squarest toe and the broadest foot and is a middle-weight shoe, the same as the Nicolini. Ultimo is less broad in the toe, with a box of shallower depth and a flat last. This is also a middle-weight shoe that is good for feet that are very flexible, since it tends to hold the foot back.

Dancers line the boxes of their pointe shoes with almost any variety of material that can be used for the purpose, but teachers and shoe manufacturers recommend lamb's wool. Not too much should be used, since a girl should be able to feel the floor when she is on pointe. Some stuff the toes of their shoes so tightly that it literally changes the size of those shoes and this should not be done.

When the time comes for a girl to go on pointe, it should be the teacher, not the parent, who chooses the shoes, and certain types of feet will be happier in certain types of shoes. For instance, a strong foot will probably not need a strong shank, which some professional dancers even break, since they do not need the support. Depending on the feet concerned, and the occasion, the pointe may be soft, medium, hard, or very hard. During the second act of *Swan Lake*, for example, it is very important for a dancer to make sure the pointe of her shoe has the hardness worn out of it to some degree. There is something rather disturbing about a flock of swans whose presence is felt as much by the sound they make on the stage as by the grace of their movements. Neither does it make any great contribution to Tchaikovsky's music. There are many ways to "wear in" the toes of pointe shoes. They are even closed in doors, hammered, or bent with the hands. Although such abusive treatment is not recommended by the manufacturers, each dancer develops her own way of suiting her shoes to her feet.

Opinions vary as to whether a child should start in a strong shoe, with the feeling being the weight of the shoe will strengthen the foot as a girl works in it, or a light shoe because then the foot must build up its own strength. At Capezio, they favor the latter. One thing emphasized at both Capezio and Freed (the two companies interviewed for this book) was that although they offer advice, they do not argue with teachers or try to force anyone whose ideas are contrary to their own to conform. To advise in the beginning is one thing, but by the time a dancer has been wearing pointe shoes for several years (and certainly by the time she has become a professional), she has developed very strong ideas about what she does and does not like. Pointe shoes are not only a very crucial part of a dancer's life, they are also a very trying one. Every pair of shoes made is unique, because it is crafted by masters, but, unfortunately, sometimes only the slightest variation in a pair of shoes can upset a dancer. This is why in the dressing room of a dancer such as Natalia Makarova there will be dozens of pairs of shoes. From these, she is constantly selecting and testing by going up on pointe in them for a few seconds, as she tries to find just the right pair for a performance. This is a common sight with all girls in ballet.

Pointe shoes have a very short life, which is most unfortunate considering how expensive they are. A ballerina during a performance of *Swan Lake* will probably go through one pair of shoes for each of the three acts in which she appears. A student, depending on how heavy she is on her shoes, and how often she takes class, may be able to make one pair last from one to three weeks.

On the subject of preserving the life of pointe shoes David Howard recommends a girl switch them from one foot to the other (as they are interchangeable) and preferably have two or three pairs she can rotate. Humidity, he says, ruins them more than anything. To help preserve the hardness in the box, dancers pour in either Fabulon or Futura floor polish and then dry the shoes.

FOUR

Judging the Teacher
POINTE WORK

One important consideration in appraising a teacher is the age at which the students start pointe work. The healthy age to start this is twelve, although some children might be allowed an occasional few minutes on pointe from the age of ten, if they have reached the right level, have exceptionally strong feet and—most important—have proficient guidance. Hyperextended* legs and sickle feet† are just two of the problems that can be caused by working in pointe shoes too early.

Once she discovers what has happened, both of these problems can cause significant technical trouble and a great deal of heartache to the girl who spends hours in front of the mirror, trying to perfect the line of her legs, and striving to develop beautifully formed feet.

There are certain feet that may be better off if they are never introduced to the pointe shoe. Just as there are many types of people suited to varying functions in life, so there are many kinds of feet suited to different capabilities. Square feet obviously have a head start, and as David Howard described it, "They can stay on pointe for a week—in fact it's almost a problem coming down." The other extreme is the poor girl with a tapered foot dancing on one toe and having to compensate greatly.

If a girl does not have a flexible foot she may be at a disadvantage if she is allowed to go on pointe at all, and may well develop problems in her Achilles tendon from the pressure created by the heel bone going into it.

Although she cannot be a ballet dancer without going on pointe,

---

* Hyperextension—a condition where the knee joint drops back. (David Howard)

† "Sickle, or sickling, a technical fault in which the foot is turned over, either inwards or outwards, from the ankle, thus breaking the line of the leg." From *The Dance Encyclopedia*.

she may become a modern dancer, or work toward jazz or folk—such as Spanish dancing—even if she only pursues it as a hobby. This also applies to the girl who may not be built for ballet. She should not necessarily give up dance altogether just because her physical attributes are inappropriate for that art.

The prospect of joining the ranks of those on pointe is always glamorous and it is only as the blisters start to come that reality hits home. This makes it doubly important, if a girl is to work correctly, that she understand the procedure ahead of time. The teacher needs

Meredith Baylis gives personal attention to a student *relevé sur les pointes en première* in pointe class at the American Ballet Center. *Photo: Steven Caras*

to pay extra attention to each student, for she is likely to be as insecure as a five-year-old child. She neither knows how to put on her pointe shoes, nor how to sew on the elastic, nor where to attach the ribbons.

So arrives the stage of: this is the way we sew on the ribbons, sew on the ribbons, sew on the ribbons, this is the way we sew on the ribbons—in the style of that well-known nursery rhyme, that takes place one cold and frosty morning.

Then girls become upset because their feet feel uncomfortable in the close-fitting shoes—again reminiscent of the Chinese lady. Hap-

At the High School for the Performing and Visual Arts in Houston, Texas, students show *passé sur pointe en écarté* at the barre. The step differs from *retiré* in that the raised foot is slightly in front of the knee before passing to the back of the standing leg and being placed again on the floor. *Photo: Mary Martha Lappe*

pily, it is not such archaic reasoning, but a necessity if a girl is to be able to benefit the most and suffer the least when she is working on pointe.

Next arrives the day of the first pointe class. One girl thinks she is going to break her ankle, while another one feels she is going to be far too tall to find a male partner, because, when on pointe, she is convinced her big feet make her much too tall. Among these, there is always the girl who is having so much fun, she wants to walk home on pointe, and the teacher ends exhausted from running back and forth, giving each dancer the individual attention so necessary at this time.

The stage at which a dancer starts to work on pointe is very crucial. Not only should her shoes be chosen for her by the teacher, but she should then be closely observed in class. As well as being sewn on the right way, the ribbons also must be tied correctly. If they are too tight, circulation will be impaired. On the other hand, if they are too loose, the shoes will not be held in place properly. The student has to learn not only to stand on pointe, but to achieve the correct positioning and line of the legs, and then also she must learn how to move. The feet must be given time to develop strength and most young girls will probably take about one year just to become familiar with the feel of the pointe shoe.

Whether or not a pupil should even be on pointe is not only important, but also sorts out the difference between the teachers who know what they are doing from those who are only interested in money. It also distinguishes between those girls who trust their teachers and those who will take class anywhere, so long as they are allowed to wear their punishing shoes. A teacher always risks losing a student who thinks she knows better than her instructor when the time is right for her to be on pointe. She is not likely to be pleased if the rest of the girls at her particular stage are all encouraged to move on, while she is left like Cinderella among the ashes, trying to hide her disappointment.

One of the toughest problems for any teacher is receiving a new girl in class who is already on pointe, and who has bent knees or hyperextended legs, and wrong placement. If a student is caught early enough, then a good instructor may be able to help her undo the damage by total retraining and allowing no pointe work until correct placement has been learned and sufficient strength built up to enable the pupil to go back on pointe and go on with the right form from there. Such retraining is not achieved overnight, but requires stamina, patience, and determination, for it could take more than a year to correct the damage. Many mild cases can be helped in this way, but there are cases of severe anatomical damage where no amount of retraining can overcome the problem and to proceed at all would only cause more harm.

Students in advanced pointe class at the San Francisco Ballet School demonstrate *relevé sur pointe en seconde arabesque. Photo: Fred Morales, Jr.*

Students in pointe class at the American Ballet Center watching attentively as Meredith Baylis demonstrates *relevé en seconde.*
Photo: Steven Caras

Basil Thompson was one of many teachers who talked about the serious injuries he had seen as a result of students being badly taught by members of the Teachers' Conventions. "There are girls who have been put on pointe at far too early an age, whose hyperextension of the legs has gone so far beyond redemption that it's almost crippling. It is obvious that the person teaching just hasn't had the required knowledge. To make it worse, the dancers themselves have not been aware of it and, sometimes, the teachers have not been either." Mr. Thompson once met a dancer who was having tremendous pains in her knees from extreme hyperextension, and he suggested that she should stop before doing more damage to her legs. Despite the fact that her legs were really deformed, and she could never have become a professional dancer, the girl left, highly insulted.

Hyperextension and sickle feet are two very good reasons a girl should not be put on pointe before the muscles and bones in the entire body are sufficiently developed, and the cartilage in the leg is fully formed. Before going on pointe, a girl should be able to stand strongly on demi-pointe* without any wavering or fluctuation in the ankle and knee joints, or the upper body and back. These things should be ingrained in the student. If the ankles and knees are loosely knit and the dancer has not developed sufficient strength, then she should definitely not be on pointe. She will only harm herself. Possibly students suffering from these problems have been on pointe from the ages of three or four because either the mother or the dance teacher thought it was cute. It is not cute. It is damaging.

Pointe Class/Variations Class/Pas de Deux Class

A student will normally not be ready to work on pointe until at least two years after she begins studying ballet. At this stage, she should probably only do pointe work about three times a week for about fifteen minutes each time, and many teachers will add that time to their ballet classes. After about one year a girl will probably build enough strength to be able to take two one-hour pointe classes a week.

* Half-pointe (up on the ball of the foot).

Pointe classes vary in format. Sometimes they will be full length ballet classes which will start at the barre and therefore require no previous warm-up. If they include boys, and girls not ready to go on pointe, the teacher will give them other steps to do, such as jumps and double tours, while those on pointe are working on their appropriate steps.

If a pointe class of one hour is taken, this should be preceded by a ballet class or at least a warm-up barre. At no time should pointe

Students in variations class at the San Francisco Ballet School in a slow movement. *Photo: Fred Morales, Jr.*

classes be considered a substitute for ballet classes, which a student should still take daily.

Those who are advanced in pointe work should take variations class. This usually lasts about an hour and will be the time when students learn variations from the classic ballets. Boys also take separate classes.

A pas de deux class is one in which the boys and girls learn to work in couples. The steps they are given to do will be those used in partnering, so that not only will they learn new movements but they will also learn the difficult technique involved.

Both these classes should be taken about twice a week by all advanced students and are of particular importance to those who have little or no opportunity to perform. David Howard emphasizes the importance of the regional companies as they give a student opportunity for stage experience. If she subsequently wishes to come to New York, with this behind her a student stands a much better chance of being accepted into a company. New York, although excellent for training, is a difficult city in which to gain performing experience, since the number of students is far in excess of the performing possibilities.

DISCIPLINE

All good teachers emphasize the need for discipline in a class, and Mme Alexandra Danilova feels anything less than the strictest discipline is totally amateurish. She firmly believes that where discipline is undermined for the sake of creativity, learning to move and freedom of expression will suffer greatly when students try to enter one of the major schools. They will find it impossible to become members of a professional company.

Professional standards simply do not make allowances for a lack of discipline, since what has to be accomplished is extensive and demanding on the pupil, and a group that is less than well organized cannot realistically be expected to achieve the standards required of a ballet dancer.

An erstwhile member of one of Europe's leading companies feels that enjoyment is also very important as discipline in these long-established companies, she feels, can be overly harsh. This does seem to be one of the prices paid by dancers in the past. It would certainly be a shame to think that such harshness is necessary for the majority so that a chosen few can emerge as great artists, leaving the impression that rigid, almost sadistic discipline is required to produce the highest caliber ballet dancers. Another ex-member of a major European com-

A class at the School of Cleveland Ballet in *tendu en arrière.* The discipline among the students in the schools is demonstrated by the photographs.

pany knows that if he tried to teach students here the way he was taught many years ago, he would be arrested for assault and battery. If he did not do a step correctly, he remembers occasions when a cane was put around his ankles. He does not remember making the same mistake twice.

Even so, there should be a serious attitude in class, and a child who takes ballet lessons in a halfhearted manner feeling that she will become a dancer will almost certainly be disappointed. There is more risk of a lackadaisical attitude away from major centers of dance, where there is neither enough competition nor any of the best training by which to compare standards. Normally a student who is receiving good training will appreciate a serious attitude in a teacher and become filled with enthusiasm. Yet, it is essential that a child, especially, feels happy in class—and wanted. It is very hard to feel happy with oneself all the time, particularly when so much energy and effort have to go into every move, and achieving the goal of the perfect line seems next to impossible. A dancer commented on how horrified she was by the faces of the students of a famous European company. "They are supposed to be doing something they love more than anything and yet, day after day, they come out of class looking depressed because nobody has given them a word of encouragement for months."

Certainly, it is important for a student to keep a sense of proportion and not to become overly depressed when she feels inadequate. When something is going wrong, she should practice and work harder, rather than think she is useless and give up too easily. "This happens all too often in this particular company," continued the dancer. "A child will say, 'I can't do it,' and the teacher will retort, 'No, you can't. I would give up if I were you.'"

HOW MUCH DOES THE TEACHER KNOW ABOUT ANATOMY?

The teacher's knowledge of anatomy is another very important element to watch out for in the classroom, and the basics, at least, are easily recognizable. Before beginning a movement, a student's body must be well aligned. That is to say the body should be completely square—as if a plumb line had been dropped from the head—with the shoulders directly over the hips and the stomach and the behind pulled in. There should be no swaybacks. However, there should be a slight, natural curve at the base of the spine, because the behind was not built to be flat either and it is bad for a dancer to be expected to achieve a straight line in this region.

If a student is forcing turnout in the legs and the teacher ignores this fact, this shows a very elementary lack of knowledge of anatomy. The toes should be facing the same direction as the kneecap, and if the feet are forced beyond this point, eventually the knees will become damaged. The turnout should be naturally developed from the hips, not forced from the feet.

Another obvious pointer to look out for are feet that roll in, or out,* at the ankles. Not only does this ruin the line of the leg, it also causes injuries.

Most people with a good eye for line should be able to identify a group that is poorly trained. If a girl is standing at the barre, pushing one straight leg up as high as it will go in front of her, and bending her other knee and arching her back, her body is being worked through tension and force. It should be developed to a point where it will be able to achieve a natural look with the one leg raised and both the other knee and the back straight.

HOW FAMILIAR IS THE TEACHER WITH FRENCH TERMINOLOGY?

Ballet teachers come in all makes and varieties, qualities—and even quantities. Many students are bewitched by their ballet instructors, whom they all too easily tend to regard as gurus who can be counted on *to do it* for them. So, a class of wide-eyed pupils is not necessarily a sign that the teacher knows what she is doing. She may not even know the French terminology but is teaching those who have no knowledge of good ballet instruction on which to base their judgment.

* When the ankles drop inward or outward.

Lack of knowledge of French terminology is indeed a negative sign. A class that is put through its paces with "benday," "stretchay," "jumpay," and "turnay" will produce dancers who will be frowned upon by any ballet company. Without the universal ballet language a teacher is forced into giving long and complicated explanations as to what is required of the dancer. When one analyzes some of the steps,

An understanding of French terminology is essential for a class to flow smoothly and here Douglas Wassell communicates easily with students at the David Howard School of Ballet. *Photo: Steven Caras*

it is easy to understand why the French terminology was adopted universally. Songsmith Tom Lehrer might well have put some of the definitions to music, had he thought of it. Certainly, they would confuse those not quite sure what they were trying to achieve.

Pas de bourrée, "a short, even, walking step by which the dancer makes progress on the stage in any given direction. In this step the movement begins with the back foot if the dancer moves forward, and with the front foot if the dancer moves backward.... Pas de bourrée may be done in innumerable ways, with or without change of feet—*dessous, dessus, couru, en tournant*, etc." (*The Dance Encyclopedia*.)

Pas de chat, "stand in fifth position, left foot front. Throw the right leg, half bent, back into 45° *croisé*, at the same time do demi-plié on the left foot. Push off with the left foot, throwing the left leg, half bent, back in *effacé* to meet the right one. There must be a moment when both feet are in the air at the same time, passing each other. Keeping the upper part of the legs turned out, and without opening them too wide, fall first on the right foot, then on the left one. The left foot passes forward into fourth position. One may finish also in fifth position." (*The Basic Principles of Classical Ballet: Russian Ballet Technique* by Agrippina Vaganova, Dover Publications, 1969.)

These definitions give some indication about how difficult the problems are for the child who has not learned the correct terminology. The surer the knowledge, the better, since companies will not give a chance to a dancer who cannot work out combinations simply by being given the names of the steps.

As Meredith Baylis firmly reminded her scholarship students one morning, "With every new contract the rehearsals get more expensive. Companies are not cheap to run." Talking on the same subject, Mme Alexandra Danilova emphasized that "if a choreographer tells them to jump through the door and they jump through the window, he may give them a second chance, but he certainly won't give them a third. I have time to teach them that in class, but he doesn't."

A company cannot afford to employ a dancer who is not capable of learning quickly; therefore a thorough knowledge of ballet language is essential.

HOW EXTENSIVE IS THE TEACHER'S DANCE VOCABULARY?

Another very important point to look out for is the extensiveness of the instructor's dance vocabulary. If only a few simple combinations are given in class, as a student progresses this limits her ability and again does not prepare her for working with choreographers. The dancer's job will also be made considerably easier if she learns to do combinations in reverse. As Mme Darvash mentioned, "Doing combinations in reverse should be standard practice in a class, yet it is amazing how many dancers become confused when asked to do this."

One reason it is beneficial to take class from a good choreographer (as long as he is also a good teacher) is that he will usually give interesting combinations. He will often use this time to create, and at the New York City Ballet Mr. Balanchine concentrates on movements he wishes to use in his choreography.

The Ballet Class and Beyond

COST

The cost of ballet lessons varies between $3.50 and $5.00 per class in most schools, although there are exceptions, and schools exist that charge higher prices. Some offer discounts which become greater as the number of classes paid for ahead of time increases. Sometimes cards for ten classes are offered, while certain schools have semester, or even annual, rates. Ironically enough, the most inexpensive place to study dance in the United States happens to be New York City.

AUDITIONS FOR ENTERING SCHOOLS

Many schools hold auditions simply to establish a child's level if she has been previously trained, as this way they can assess which group she should be studying with. In the case of most schools, the only time a pupil is likely to be rejected is either if previous bad training has caused her to develop physical problems, or if they are using the Soviet method of selection and choosing only those who appear to have ideal potential for becoming professional ballet dancers, such as at the School of American Ballet.

Since standards can change from year to year, it is not possible to endorse schools in this book, even though many of them currently have excellent reputations, as for example those mentioned here. It is hoped the reader interested in examining local schools will be helped in making his own judgment by using this book as a guide. It is not even possible to establish a rule of thumb for schools, since a building with chandeliers set in spacious grounds does not necessarily mean that the standards of dance teaching will be high. A private teacher tucked away in the corner of some shopping center may be a first-rate instructor.

WHERE TO BEGIN STUDYING

The consensus of all teachers does seem to be that, with rare exceptions, it is not worth studying ballet in a little school way out in the country. If it is possible for a child to take some kind of free-style dancing or even tap, this is what she should do until she can move to a big city. It is simply not worth trusting a teacher whose knowledge is inadequate. If a child is definitely going to take ballet, there is no reason why she should not start at the age of twelve. She will be far better off waiting until she is that age, and beginning with a good teacher, than starting off badly at a younger age where a great deal of damage might be done.

ADVANCEMENT
IN BALLET TRAINING

Training in ballet is advancing with the times and one could say that in some areas it has been almost revolutionized by certain teachers. David Howard is one who teaches completely differently from the manner in which he was taught in England. Although the basic steps and patterns of the arms are the same, he believes that nowadays teachers are learning to be more sympathetic to the needs of the dancer, rather than sticking with the idea that if it worked for a famous ballerina, it will work for any dancer. With ballet training being as tough as it is, in the old days, it was probably only those with nerves and bodies of steel who made it through the net of severity that seems to have engulfed all the great established European ballet schools. Even dancers as young as thirty years of age remember being ordered to stick at something until they did it right, which they did—

David Howard demonstrates first arabesque to an attentive class at his school. *Photo: Steven Caras*

from sheer fear. Still, the idea of questioning a teacher's methods or principles was unheard of unless a student was happy with the prospect of no future in the ballet world.

Like the student, a good teacher is always learning, and will develop her methods according to the demands of the dancer. It is now accepted that there is more than one way to produce the same result and a teacher with a good eye will be able to look at a dancer who is having difficulty doing a particular step and be able to suggest an alternative approach.

TEACHER'S ABILITY
TO COMMUNICATE IDEAS

David Howard takes the kinesthetic approach to ballet and finds that in trying to communicate his ideas there can be problems. To deal with words when the end result must be movement can lead to confusion, as he has discovered. For example, he would say that the body does not muscularly "pull up," but it "counterstretches." Most people consider it to be the same thing, yet, Mr. Howard says, "It might look the same, but it doesn't feel the same. Try putting your leg out in front of you and pointing your foot. That is how a lot of instruction is given. Now, if you think of it differently, as sending energy through to your foot causing it to stretch, your thigh has to react as a result. In other words, you've caused the foot to move, you haven't done it as an isolated movement. Many ballet teachers will tell you that's pulling up, but it isn't. It's a completely different feeling muscularly. You're dealing with muscular reaction, rather then blindly following an order." At this stage, many people have come to appreciate Mr. Howard's approach.

WORKING
WITH DIFFERENT TEACHERS

Taking class from different teachers is also considered to be beneficial, provided they are all teachers with a good reputation, and this can be achieved within a company school, for example. Although the various teachers are working under the same umbrella of their respective directors, they will have their own individual teaching methods, and this will enable a dancer to develop an idea of the kind of teaching that works best for her. Alternatively, a dancer can indulge a sound, if less than cornucopian, choice by trying the various independent teachers and finding the one best suited to her needs, at any given time. If a dancer is gaining the maximum from working with any one teacher, then it is probably better if she remains in one place for as long as she feels the benefit.

Sometimes a dancer will become so attached to a teacher that she will not want to change or take supplementary classes from another teacher even if necessary. Too much trust is the fault of that teacher in allowing the pupil to overly depend on her and maybe even encouraging her to do so, rather than showing the pupil how to function independently. This most often occurs in the case of a talented student and sometimes teachers become unhealthily possessive. A student is then very limited since her outlook on dance becomes formed and colored according to one teacher's opinions and ideas. It is very important for a student to have exposure to every aspect of the dance, including other good teachers, even if their schools of thought may vary from that of her own instructor. This way a student can learn from them and can develop her own sense of perspective.

A teacher to guard against is one who insists that she is the only good instructor available in a given area, even if her training happens to be good and work for many people. While that may be true away from major centers of dance, it certainly would not be true where dance teachers proliferate, such as in New York City. The dance teacher who talks in this negative way to young students only encourages them to become closed-minded; apart from which, it is totally unprofessional. Just as there are many different body types, so there are different ways of teaching and it is important that each student find what works best for her. If a student trusts a particular teacher and attends her classes regularly, she is not likely to leave. However, there may be a particular point a dancer is having difficulty

with and she will need a teacher who specializes in her weakness. Possibly she needs to improve her jumping or turning. Many times a teacher cannot give a student everything she needs and the object is for the student to dance to the best of her ability. She is the one who is working toward being a performer, not the teacher. A student who finds herself in this situation can still go to such a teacher, if she is benefiting from the training, but she should not allow herself to be run by that teacher. If it reaches the point where a teacher's possessiveness is becoming stifling, certainly a student should look elsewhere.

CHANGING TEACHERS

A dancer should also learn to recognize when it is time to change teachers. This can occur either because she is with a teacher not well suited to her in the first place or because she has reached a point where her particular teacher can no longer be of help to her. This is why it is always of benefit to at least observe various teachers and talk to students to find out other teachers' ways of working. This way, if the time arrives when a student wants to change teachers, it is less likely to be such a dramatic step. Such situations occur all the time, and do not necessarily indicate a fault either on the part of the student or the teacher—simply that the time has come to move on.

ADVANTAGES OF FORMER DANCER AS TEACHER

Although there are exceptions, where advanced students or professional dancers are concerned, most teachers feel it is very important for them to be taught by someone who has had experience as a

---

Basil Thompson demonstrates the positions of the feet and the technique used in *entrechat* at the American Ballet Center. *Photo: Steven Caras*

professional dancer, because otherwise a person cannot be fully aware of what it is like to move onstage. Only after that experience is one fully cognizant of the demands that are made on a dancer, can gauge a student's progress, and also know how to work with her when she is performing. This requires great sensitivity. A teacher should be aware of how much pressure can be put on a person under

Former prima ballerina Alexandra Danilova passes on her knowledge to students in a variations class at the School of American Ballet. (Readers may recognize her as the coach Mme Dakarova in the film *The Turning Point.*) *Photo: Steven Caras*

these circumstances, and which days to permit the dancer to go through a class without working as hard as usual. There are even days when a student might just take a barre to warm up, then leave the class, if she is in the middle of a heavy performance schedule.

As was emphasized by Mme Danilova, now teaching at the School of American Ballet: "I have a vivid memory of what I went through and therefore I am able to teach them to pay attention to very crucial areas. If you haven't danced, how can you possibly understand the stamina it takes to get through a hard performance, and help a dancer develop a sense of this? Mr. Balanchine knows I drive them because I realize they have to do it. However, at the age of fifteen or sixteen they have a hard time keeping a sense of proportion and I tell them especially to be careful, because they can't go to Saks [Fifth Avenue] and buy another pair of legs. It is better to underdo than overdo."

Of course, with a very gifted dancer, there can also be drawbacks when teaching. Patricia Wilde suffered from the problem of a body that was too loose and turned out as a child and she was one of the rare few who had to learn to tighten and control it. She finds she really has to be aware of how difficult it is for the majority of students who have to fight very hard to loosen their bodies and develop a turnout.

MASTER CLASSES

On the subject of master classes, it is generally agreed that the principal benefit is that they are an eye-opener, rather than reliable as a day-to-day class, and Ms. Wilde talked of this. A visiting teacher, who may give half a dozen classes, is able to show a student the correct way to work, but will not be in a position to see if she is able to maintain her standard on the level that is taught to her. Most teachers agree with the instructor who stated, "A teacher's theory cannot work without her being present, because each one has her own individual way of working." Many of the best teachers have followers who have learned to teach their methods.

Master classes compare in some respects to setting a long-running play. Once the director leaves, the play becomes more and more wrinkled as it ages, until the director returns to give it a face-lift. Although the play will simply become tired, a dancer may develop a wrong method of working on a particular step.

If a student's regular teacher has been giving a certain correction that the student is questioning for some reason, it can be of great benefit to hear it from a second teacher, at which point the student is more likely to pay attention. On the other hand, if a pupil is really stuck over a position or movement, and her own instructor has not been able to reach her, a second teacher might be able to help by describing that particular point in a different way.

TEACHER/PARENT RELATIONSHIP

Barbara Thuesen emphasizes the personal touch with any student. A parent should discuss his child's body type with the teacher, and be able to understand any special problems the child might have. For instance, if a child is knock-kneed or bowlegged, she should be carefully watched. The teacher should keep a careful check on progress and be able to stop the child doing any exercise for which she may not be ready. As long as that student is not given a feeling she is a failure, because she cannot move as fast as other pupils, there is no reason for the situation to become traumatic. If she is convinced she just has to develop more slowly to build strength, there is no reason for any kind of setback.

MUSIC TRAINING

If a child shows a sign of really enjoying her ballet classes, this is also a good age to start her with some kind of music training, because a good knowledge of the rudiments of music is important. Even if musicality is inherent in an individual, it is considerably more difficult to dance with true musicality if a dancer is not intimate with the way music is structured. In all the world's leading European ballet schools musical training is an essential part of the curriculum. Many people who are entering a child into dance class are unaware of how greatly a knowledge of music will facilitate the child's understanding of the whole concept of dance.

Mr. Balanchine is a choreographer known for his musicality and he will never allow music to be changed. If a dancer is having difficulty fitting a certain piece of choreography to its accompanying music, he will adapt the choreography, but never allow the conductor to adapt to the dancer.

TEACHER'S KNOWLEDGE OF MUSIC

It is not only the dancers who lack a good knowledge of music. Barbara Thuesen talked of that knowledge as being one of the definite ways in which a teacher could be tested, and cited one particular case of a famous dancer who has now become a teacher. She saw him ask his pianist to play a waltz, and when the pianist complied he promptly told him that was wrong and started humming a mazurka. (As David Howard explained, the basic difference between the two is where the accent falls on the music.)

It is not uncommon for a pianist in a class to have to follow the students, rather than the other way around—and often the teacher will raise no objection because he may well not be aware of what is happening. One morning in class Mme Darvash was working with a new pianist as her own proficient accompanist, Maria Raffa, was sick. At one point, the lady at the piano started to follow the dancers in the professional class, as they worked hard on perfecting a combination. Probably, she was like so many pianists who find it easier to work that way but Mme Darvash did not approve. "Don't follow them," was the polite request. "That way they'll never learn to listen to the music."

Many teachers, not in a position to afford a pianist, learn a certain amount about music from records. For example, a record may indicate that the pliés are accompanied by a waltz in that instance. This is a

very poor way to acquire a knowledge of music and inadequate knowledge can cause problems in a dance class. It is usually a sign that the teacher herself received poor ballet training, or at least poor musical instruction.

TEACHER'S SENSE OF HUMOR/ TEACHER AS PSYCHOLOGIST

One of the bonuses that encourages a student who is earnestly pushing herself through ballet class is her teacher's good sense of humor. This is something that several of them have in abundance, and although the work that is going on must be taken seriously, their dry remarks can certainly give a lift to the class. It also helps to alleviate the somewhat military air that can be created by these ethereal sergeant majors.

Mme Darvash tried to keep the professional class moving one morning after a holiday weekend. "So, shall I take it with the music once, being Monday? You know it really. You just want me to take a class too. . . . I told you, turn your head, young lady. You don't need a stiff head in order to think. You can think with your head in any position. . . . And you, especially, after going to the disco, keep your hip down." When the barre work was over and the portable barres needed to be carried off, she addressed the class: "We have our *cavalieri* to take the barres away and makes us feel like ladies. I don't believe in women's lib. To become President, yes, but to work three times as hard as before, no."

David Howard has a similar way of keeping up the tempo even at the end of a day, as he demonstrated during an advanced beginners' class. "Which arm is going to go up first? Think. You have many

Patricia Wilde is demonstrating *grand jeté en avant* Bournonville style to scholarship students at the American Ballet Theatre School. *Photo: Steven Caras*

arms—as you are showing me—pick one! We'll go with the right and the left, and *glissade*,* and again." Later, the students stood to the side of the studio tracing a combination he was demonstrating with the familiar hand movements used. "Now don't just stand there knitting with your hands, that won't do any good. It has to come from the head." Then, as they started to move again, "And lift—everything, not just the eyebrows." Later, to a man, trying to get the correct position in attitude,† "This is ballet—not a yoga advertisement." After giving the students another step he continues, "Now let's start with the single—your security blanket. Now the magic of the double." As the class ends, another is scheduled to begin. The waiting crowd rushes on to the floor, spreading out to take their favorite places at the barre, as if having to take another spot would mean disaster.

At the American Ballet Center, Meredith Baylis puts the scholarship students through a combination. "Now that means nothing, because your arms were nonexistent. Do you think people want to pay top ticket prices to see that?" They continue, and then, "You know something? You're dull. Now I see the corners of the mouth going up. I may be evil, but I like to be entertained."

In this way, a good teacher must also be part psychologist. It is very necessary to understand what it takes to motivate each student, as well as knowing how to keep day-to-day order.

GAUGING PROGRESS

It is very important for a dancer to be able to gauge her progress from year to year because nobody else can do this for her. Signs to watch out for are bulky muscles—if the legs start to become overdeveloped then something is wrong, unless the family's physical makeup is stocky. Then there is nothing that any amount of ballet training will do to change the physique itself. Even so the individual can learn

* "A gliding step; a preparatory movement for leaps." From *The Dance Encyclopedia*.

† "A pose wherein one leg is raised in back, well bent at the knee. Usually the same arm as leg is raised. In front attitude the working leg is raised in front, knee slightly bent, opposite arm raised." From *The Dance Encyclopedia*.

to work in such a way as to create an illusion with her body. Apart from those with a stocky build, nowadays, especially, a body that is properly trained will have elongated muscles.

A person should watch good dancers and develop her eye for line. If she sees they can accomplish certain things she is still unable to do after years of training, then it should be obvious something is seriously wrong.

Dennis Nahat, a director of the Cleveland Ballet, talks of a girl who appeared at one of that company's auditions. She traveled a great distance to New York convinced that she was of the caliber taken by major ballet companies. When dancing she looked less appealing than she did in street clothes, whereas it should have been just

Students attempting *grand jeté en avant* Bournonville style as demonstrated by Patricia Wilde in scholarship class at the American Ballet Theatre School. *Photo: Steven Caras*

the opposite. A dancer should exude beauty—the whole face should be lit up—and the movements should be clean. This particular girl had been dancing for thirteen years and yet was totally unaware she was doing everything wrong. She had obviously never checked her progress and so Mr. Nahat asked her to stand aside and watch the other girls who came after her. She stood there for a while and then went up to him. "It's all right, you don't have to say anything more. I see the difference." She left utterly devastated.

AUDITIONS FOR ENTERING COMPANIES

Once a student reaches a certain standard, then comes the time she will be ready to audition. This is something faced by all dancers, but for those lucky enough to have been taught by the company schools, in which case, if they are good enough, and are working toward entering that particular company, there is a chance they will be asked to join it after being watched by the appropriate people in company class or possibly a performance.

David Howard has advice to give to those facing auditions: girls should have their hair neatly tied back and should not wear nail polish. Boys should be sure to have their hair well cut, since tidiness is a very important aspect of professionalism. Students should wear colors that flatter them, taking into consideration that company directors and ballet masters will be looking at their bodies as well as their work. Also companies look beyond technical capabilities. They may be looking for dancers to fill very specific roles, and even particular costumes, which these days cost a great deal of money. If a dancer can be found who will fit into an already existing wardrobe, this will certainly be taken into consideration by the company directors. Sometimes a company will be looking for a dancer of a certain height and hair color, but a student is well advised to try as many auditions as possible, simply to be seen and to take advantage of the experience.

A dancer should appear self-confident when facing an audition, no matter how nervous she may be inside. One who can do this shows herself much more likely to be able to face a different audience every night. She is also more likely to be the one who will make it through a performance in emergencies such as having to dance, at a moment's notice, a part she barely knows. There is something most appealing about a dancer who moves around with a certain sense of urgency. It is such a small point, but that first impression as the dancer steps onstage is so important. She should also keep her confidence at the end—no matter whether or not she feels she has given a good audition. At least if she can finish with presence, she will not show the people watching the audition that she has any negative feelings. It will also be necessary if she makes a mistake in a performance later on to be able to carry through with an air that indicates that nothing has gone wrong. To enter and leave with strength are not just basic skills, they are obvious psychological pluses, and in an audition there is usually only one chance. Also, the dancer who has the guts to try something first, in the event of a choice, is showing a positive attitude.

Most auditions take the form of a class rather than a stage appearance, and the dancers that a company would like to consider may be asked to come back more than once.

PERFORMING

Meredith Baylis maintains that a dancer should start performing once she has reached a certain point in her training, for otherwise she will only become class-stale. She will then start to manufacture problems, instead of finishing her technique onstage, which must be done, since there is a certain technique that can never be developed in class.

Moving on to a new phase in anything is rarely easy, and one of the best possible excuses is to procrastinate. It also serves as the perfect excuse if something does not go well, like the dancer who falls off pirouette looking down at the floor as if to transfer the blame.

It is of some significance for a child to begin dance classes with a teacher who will be able to put her in performances. For example, the

A company apprentice rehearsal class at the School of the Pennsylvania Ballet, showing fish-dive. In the foreground are Sari Braff (apprentice) and Ty Granaroli (company member). *Photo: Mildred Keil*

Students watch earnestly as rehearsal takes place at the Cleveland Ballet. The girl is in fourth arabesque. *Photo: Alexander Aitken*

A curtain call after a performance of *A Sense of Wonder,* showing students of the Stone Camryn School of Ballet in Chicago. *Photo: Paul Hansen*

School of American Ballet has an annual workshop each May, and children from the school also appear on stage with the New York City Ballet in such ballets as *Harlequinade, The Nutcracker,* and *A Midsummer Night's Dream.* Children from the American Ballet Theatre School appear in ballets such as *Études, La Sylphide,* and *Petrouchka* with American Ballet Theatre. Although *Petrouchka* is an example of a ballet where the children appear, but do not actually dance, at least it gives them a sense of awareness of stage presence. Many careful hours go into rehearsing these children, and at the School of American Ballet, David Richardson, himself a dancer with the New York City Ballet, tempers endless patience with just the right amount of discipline. In many other areas throughout the United States dance schools are similarly involved with other companies, both large and small. Many more do not work with companies, but put on their own productions a few times a year.

If a child is going to take ballet seriously, then the younger she starts onstage the better. This will build her self-confidence for she will begin to develop a feeling of movement and she will not have the shock of facing an audience for the first time when she is older.

Performances give added interest, since the child feels some sense of what it is to be a ballet dancer. They give her a feeling of what all those tedious exercises are for and provide incentive for her to improve.

It is hard for a young child to go to class day after day, and even

Students feel a sense of achievement when able to perform. Here some of them rehearse at Stone Camryn School of Ballet studio.

though performing is not a way by which she can gauge her progress in the exact sense, through it she will feel she is achieving something.

Even for the child who is taking preballet, if a school works on a production that can include her at the age of six or seven, as a butter-fly or a bird in a walk-on part, it will give that child an awareness of the stage.

DANCERS' SCHEDULES

The demands on a dancer these days are excessive. American Ballet Theatre now goes into rehearsal in August for the New York season in September at the Metropolitan Opera House. They then go back into rehearsal, before leaving for a one-month visit to Washington, D.C., in December, followed by a three-month tour covering most of the country, before returning to New York in April for their two- to three-month spring season. The company is guaranteed forty working weeks a year, with some of the free time being fitted into the annual schedule.

An example of the New York City Ballet schedule is a fourteen-week winter season in New York, then a two-month tour, and a two-month spring season at home. This is followed by three weeks in Saratoga Springs, New York, in July, and afterward there is often a trip abroad. This company has very few weeks of vacation each year.

On top of this, many members of these and other companies make guest appearances during the seasons, as well as during their "vacation" period. For dancers there is very little true vacation, for they must continue to take class to keep their bodies in shape. Gary Chryst, of the Joffrey Ballet, once broke his foot in class, during a time the company was not performing. The insurance company involved queried the situation, saying they could not comprehend why he needed to take class at such a time. The reason is that dancers are artistic athletes and not people lucky enough to be born with special gifts, who enjoy going onstage to show their prowess. Anthony Dowell spent a year as a member of American Ballet Theatre, and continues as guest artist. He mentioned that the doctors at his home company (Great Britain's Royal Ballet) recommend at least four weeks' vacation—two weeks to unwind followed by two weeks for the body to start preparing itself for the grind ahead. Normally, he finds this works very well, although immediately prior to beginning his year with American Ballet Theatre, he was with the Royal Ballet in Greece, then stayed on for a vacation before coming to New York to dance in *Giselle*. Feeling the importance of the upcoming performance, he continued to work during that time, to the accompaniment of a tape of one of the Royal Ballet's pianists. He stated ironically, "I religiously did a barre every day, which is something I've never done in the holidays. It's not much fun being in Greece where everyone is out on the beach, and there you are pushing back the bed of your hotel room to give yourself enough room to work with."

BALLET IS HARD WORK

Teachers are consistently hitting their students with truths, such as the reminder from Meredith Baylis: "This is where you decide if you want to work that hard to be paid that little. I will not paint a grand and glorious picture. Absolutely the most difficult thing to do is get into a company. Then your work starts, unless you're going to be satisfied to be the last one in the line. As you climb the ladder, you've always got some youngster coming along behind you and that's where your artistry and maturity have to stand for you, together with your years of work. The person coming up behind you may have a leg that goes higher or be able to do more turns, but is she the artist you are? That is what you have to think of."

On the subject of working hard, Mme Darvash added, "The problem with most pupils is they like to take a class, but they don't like to study. For that reason, many teachers adapt to them, rather than the other way around. If I felt a teacher couldn't teach me anything I wouldn't want to go to him. So, you talk to them and hope that little by little they understand. The big question is always whether they want to be professionals or whether they want one to fool them to make them feel better."

Robert Barnett watches closely at the Atlanta Ballet as work is carried out on the art of partnering and being partnered. The girl is in an intermediate position, executing *développé écarté*. (The bent leg will straighten.) The man is in *quatrième croisé*. *Photo: Jill Fineberg*

Of course, the student who wants to be a dancer badly enough will have both the sense of urgency and the desire to fight for the chance.

David Howard also feels anybody who wants to be a successful dancer will somehow make sure she searches out the people who can help her, but does not think that success should be judged only on whether or not a person becomes a professional. Many just enjoy taking class and doing the occasional performance without having any intention of allowing dance to become life. Even a successful dancer should keep a sense of proportion and not allow herself to become swallowed up by the profession, and someone who appears to practice this belief is Mikhail Baryshnikov. When asked on CBS's "60 Minutes," "Why do you dance?" he replied, quite simply, "It's my job."

Homework
READING

Reading about dance technique definitely has its advantages, although those advantages should not be considered a panacea. It is one thing to read about the correct way to point the foot, but quite another thing to put it into practice. The way some books are written, as with the way some teachers express themselves, may make perfect sense to one person, yet be quite unclear to another. One afternoon, a pupil of Mme Darvash approached her and referred to another teacher, who, the girl said, talked in the same way as Madame herself. "Oh, she did? Well, you know I could repeat what Edison said, but never invent the light bulb," was Madame's reply.

Reading material can be a good guide as to whether or not a student is receiving the right instruction, because it explains the right and wrong way of doing things and gives a student a sense of proportion. If a girl has been studying dance for five years and cannot do a good pirouette, something is wrong. Written matter also explains the reasons for doing particular steps, and how strength is built. However, a student should not try to teach herself to dance simply by reading or allow a teacher to instruct her that way either, because then it becomes a routine. An instructor must have her own theories and her own way of working and if she does not, it is an indication that she is not sure of the reasons behind her teaching. Even if she is following a good instruction manual, it is as bad as a teacher who knows little or nothing about ballet. If she does not understand the reasons for each movement, a teacher obviously has no idea of the total concept of ballet training. An instructor cannot simply teach the routine of a combination, he must understand what it is intended to achieve. It is the application that is important.

It is also important to be sure of the credentials of the author of the book one is reading. Most good teachers are able to list a number of reliable authors, although the ones they recommend will vary according to their own theories.

The National Association for Regional Ballet* is a very capable nonprofit organization familiar with teaching standards and schools throughout the United States, and can be consulted for advice by those who need it. The N.A.R.B. has a membership of approximately 120 dance companies, and works closely with them in establishing and maintaining high standards both in training and in the companies themselves.

Another source of reference is *Dancemagazine*,† which is published monthly and contains a wealth of information for people interested or involved in the dance. Apart from very good feature articles on individual dancers, there are reviews, information on newly created ballets, plus articles on everything from teachers in the Russian tradition to eating a balanced diet, and from the steps to the Ballet Russe version of the "Dance of the Sugar Plum Fairy" variation from Tchaikovsky's *Nutcracker*, to details of who is dancing where. As its name implies, *Dancemagazine* is not simply restricted to ballet, and the list of schools and companies it advertises is very extensive. This will give the reader an idea of what is available in her area, and for further information she can then contact the N.A.R.B.

Purely from the viewpoint of interesting articles and up-to-date coverage, another good monthly magazine is *Ballet News*.†† There is also a monthly newspaper that supplies exactly what its name implies—*Dance News*.§ For those wishing to learn the movements that go with the appropriate French terminology, there is a book called the *Technical Manual and Dictionary of Classical Ballet*, by Gail Grant.**

*N.A.R.B., 1860 Broadway, New York, N.Y. 10023. President, Norman Fagan; Executive Director, Doris Hering.

† *Dancemagazine*, Danad Publishing Co., Inc., 1180 Avenue of the Americas, New York, N.Y. 10036.

†† *Ballet News* is published by the Metropolitan Opera Guild, Inc., 1865 Broadway, New York, N.Y. 10023. Subscriptions: *Ballet News,* Subscription Service Dept., Box 918, Farmingdale, N.Y. 11737.

§ Dance News, Inc., 119 West 57 Street, New York, N.Y. 10019.

**This book is published by Dover Publications, Inc., 180 Varick Street, New York, N.Y. 10014.

There are a great many dance critics writing throughout the United States, and the Dance Critics' Association* will be able to offer information about them. Alternatively, they are listed in *Dancemagazine Annual*. While critics supply valuable information about ballet, once again a person should be prepared to keep an open mind, rather than regarding a critic's word as definitive. He will review a ballet according to his own knowledge and taste, which may or may not coincide with that of the reader, who should use the writer's word simply as a guide from which to form his own opinions. Some of the established critics also write books and articles on many aspects of ballet and the people involved in it, which supply valuable information and can make interesting reading.

PRACTICING AT HOME

Capable teachers feel that any practicing a student does at home should be suggested by the instructor, who will then be able to keep an eye on the results. Every pupil battles with her own individual problems and should therefore be given personal attention. As David Howard explains, "One always feels freer at home than in the studio, and I feel some of the fantasies and frustrations should be got out of the body. I think you should point your feet, stretch your arms and look at yourself but not dance all day long at home. A student should work on improving herself, because two hours a day is not long enough."

He does not feel that a definite time for these exercises should be given, because if a child is watched over every day until she manages to do something correctly, she will probably become totally disenchanted.

One way for a mother to understand her child's own problems is for her to watch classes occasionally, so she can develop her own eye. If she is prepared to work with the teacher and the child, a great deal can be accomplished.

A parent must be careful to remain objective and trust the teacher. Whatever happens, she should not give corrections to her child

---

* Dance Critics Association, P.O. Box 47, Planetarium Station, New York, N.Y. 10024.

during a class, since this is one of the best ways to promote the teacher's antagonism. Apart from this, many parents will give wrong corrections, particularly if their knowledge is just gleaned from watching teachers. Also it is disruptive to the rest of the class.

Turnout can be worked on independently, because it can be helped while a child is concentrating on something else. The way to do this is by sitting in frog position* on the floor while doing homework, for example. This way the mind is preoccupied and turnout is actually being developed with the body in a relaxed position. In this manner the pelvis is squared off automatically, and the turnout from the hip socket will be correct. Sometimes a child may feel inclined to hold the same position while lying on her back. This is all right if she is not watching television; from that position the angle is bad enough to put a strain on the eyes.

Exercises such as spotting the head and stretching can be worked on but this should be done under the teacher's guidance.

LIVING A FULL LIFE/ WATCHING PERFORMANCES/ FILM/TELEVISION

One of the most effective ways of doing homework is for the child to lead as full a life as possible and observe what is going on around her. If she visits museums, goes on nature walks, paints, or rides a bicycle she will be able to draw on such things when she is dancing because the more knowledge she has of life, the more she will begin to question and create, and her ability as a dancer will be enhanced.

If a child is in a position to take acting classes it will be to her advantage, and it is recommended that she acquire a knowledge of acting if she wishes to become a professional dancer.

A girl in *A Chorus Line* devoted an entire song to telling the world how she had "felt nothing," while having to pretend she was an ice-

---

* Frog position is achieved by putting the bottoms of the feet together and pulling the heels in toward the pelvis.

cream cone or a tobogganer in acting class, though this somewhat un-popular aspect of the training impressed the lyricist sufficiently for him to write a song about it.

Gary Chryst disliked having to take such classes. He remembers having to make the face of a camel, and being a very talented mimic, he still does it most convincingly, by sucking in his cheeks and rolling his eyes. On occasion he had to imitate an eggbeater, but at the time of talking about it, the broken foot he had sustained in ballet class precluded a demonstration that would no doubt have been just as effective.

While observing the world around her, it is also important for a child to see as many performances as possible—including modern, jazz, and other forms of dance. If she lives in the country, and the only live performances she has a chance to see are local recitals, she should also watch dance on television. This will help to develop her eye and give her a sense of appreciation of what she should try to achieve. Many dance companies, both American and foreign, are shown regularly on television these days. All these companies have their own special dancers and their unique points from which a student, or even another dancer, can learn. In this way, she will be exposed to the various grades of performance.

The filming of dance has its controversial aspects; when the two art forms, dance and film, are brought together, both have to be somewhat compromised. Usually the camera is either too close or too far back. Ballet is a very refined art, and the acting and mime are very subtle, so if the camera is too far away all that is missed. On the other hand, if it is shot from up close, it becomes overly intimate, and the overall illusion is lost.

Ballets are often adapted to some extent for the camera, which in turn is compromised because it is used as an instrument to deliver dance in the best possible fashion to the audience, rather than having the free range that its own enormous capacity affords. Witness to that is a stunning photograph of an area of Jupiter, taken from three million miles away, which could have passed as a close-up of an oil slick on the Hudson River. This is one way in which film can create its own illusion and atmosphere, which it must do to compensate for the old adage that nothing is as good as being there.

Movies of the great dancers can be fun to watch, beginning with the earliest films available. These can be viewed by appointment only at the Dance Research Department of the library at Lincoln Center for the Performing Arts in New York City, but viewing is restricted. Although the Soviet films can be seen by anyone, showing great artists such as Galina Ulanova, films of most American and European companies are limited, for union reasons, to those learning the parts.

In a discussion on films from which dancers could learn the parts, Peter Martins talked of the difficulties of learning a role in this way. "You are constantly having to turn your back to a film, so that you can watch it over your shoulder to get the steps the right way around." Dancers, he said, always learn a role from another dancer by watching from behind and then added that it would be ideal for them if films could be shot that way.

Looking at films made over the years it can be seen how the technique in ballet has progressed. The demands now are so severe that a *corps de ballet* member is capable of greater technical achievements than the principals of years gone by. However, even though the technique may have improved, the one aspect that will always shine through with the erstwhile great ballet dancers is their artistry. That is one characteristic that no amount of technical refinement can surpass, no matter of what era the dancer.

One film that is available to the public is the oldest ballet movie known to exist. This is the *Royal Danish Ballet, 1902–1906.** The film uses footage shot by the Danish court photographer, Peter Elfelt, and is actually several short films spliced together and recently fitted to music. An article† in *Dancemagazine* describes the movie. "Much of the dancing is brilliant by any standard: the pointe work sharp and precise, the beats clean and quick, the *enchaînements*†† controlled and effectively shaped.

"The film also shows how well the Danes have preserved the Bournonville heritage. Much of the material of this seventy-five-year-old film is being danced almost exactly the same way today."

* The 16mm film (14 min., b/w, sound) can be rented for $20, purchased for $240, from Dance Film Archive, University of Rochester, Rochester, N.Y. 14627.

† *"The Oldest Ballet Movie"* by John Mueller, *Dancemagazine*, July 1979.

†† Linking. A combination of two or more steps arranged to fit a phrase of music.

SEVEN

Keeping the Balance

THE HOME LIFE
OF A CHILD IN THE ARTS

A parent who has a child involved in the arts, especially one who is talented, needs to take many points into consideration with regard to that child's home life.

To begin with, there is the question of how to tell whether a child has talent, then how to nurture it without making the child feel different. If a parent wishes a child to dance, Dr. Rocco John La Manna, Senior Child Psychologist at Coney Island Hospital, feels that the initial way to test a child's interest is by exposing her to music and dance, then watching her reaction. In the event the child is very coordinated and musical, she may show an interest in ballet. If the desire and the talent are strong enough, they will come through, but the environment can also be conducive.

A child enrolled in a ballet class may show a serious interest and have the ability to pick things up, but only when she grows older can it be proven whether or not she has the makings of a ballet dancer. Her body will not really be set until she goes through puberty, and before this time it will not be possible to tell what her physical make-up will be. One can only guess by observing the build of her parents.

However, David Howard feels that parents should keep a sense of proportion here. Some mothers tend to bring in a daughter who simply has an irresistible urge to jump up and dance round the television set every time there is music. At this point the mother sometimes becomes very excited and thinks this means her daughter has the potential of Anna Pavlova. Almost all young children will have some inclination to dance to music and as Mr. Howard explains, "It's the ones who never react to music at all that you're more inclined to worry about." Unless the girl who does constantly move to music has a sense of what she is doing, it probably does not indicate anything more than a natural urge to respond to the music.

Parents who are living with a talented child may also be subject to tantrums with unpleasing regularity, and think they have to make allowances for "artistic temperament." Dr. La Manna disagrees with this, and he talks of a famous study once done on gifted children by Dr. Louis B. Terman, which is regarded as the definitive study by authorities. Dr. Terman studied gifted children from a very early age into adulthood—an unusually long-term survey—and his findings shattered many of the beliefs held until then. Certainly, the gifted were different from other children. Most of them had fewer problems, physically, were less shy and introverted, and basically very well adjusted. They were leaders, involved in more activities, and their achievements tended to be greater.

Although this survey seems to tell much about talented people, it was not enough to wash away the belief that an artistic temperament goes hand in hand with talent. Dr. La Manna believes people like stereotypes because once something is categorized they feel safe in dealing with it. Once the idea of the artistic temperament was established, all it needed was the occasional star to manifest herself in this way for the stereotype to remain. Yet there are few stories that reach the newspapers to support it. The famous case of Sallie Wilson, principal dancer with American Ballet Theatre, throwing a glass of Scotch in the face of Clive Barnes* was as much a display of genuine anger, as a mood of the moment. The incident happened after Marcia Haydée, a principal with the Stuttgart Ballet, had danced *Fall River Legend*, a ballet that Mr. Barnes had admitted he did not like. Despite this, he had always praised Sallie Wilson in the role, one for which she had become noted all over the world, having danced it for eleven years. In mentioning the great exponents of the ballet, Mr. Barnes named Nora Kaye and Alicia Alonso, praised Marcia Haydée for her performance, and refrained from mentioning Sallie Wilson. As Sallie stated, "He just simply cut out eleven years of my career." Mr. Barnes apparently

---

* Then dance and theater critic of the *New York Times*; now of the *New York Post*.

felt Ms. Wilson's reaction to be justified. When on a lecture tour the following year, during the question-and-answer period, this was invariably the first question that would be raised, and his reaction was always one of amusement. He would talk of the incident favorably—and dancer and critic are now on good terms.

If a child does tend to erupt very easily, Dr. La Manna thinks the parents should take a careful look at the child's life to see what is frustrating her and, if necessary, question their own motivations as to the way they are handling her life. For instance, are the parents reinforcing what the child wants to do, rather than putting their own expectations onto her? If a girl's mother is a frustrated dancer then maybe she is trying to push her daughter to fulfill thwarted ambition. Depending on the child, many things can then happen. She may become an overachiever and perform way above her capabilities, or she may rebel and go in totally the opposite direction.

Quite often an only child will tend to be an overachiever. Maybe it is a result of the attention, or of the pushing, and both parents putting all their expectations and hopes on the shoulders of the child, but these children are also the ones most often referred to guidance counselors. They may achieve, but they pay the price.

Preferably a child should be exposed to a wide variety of situations. The parents should watch her response carefully and then follow through by supporting the child's inclinations, rather than pushing her into something for which she has no real enthusiasm.

When a child is pushed from a very young age, all kinds of problems can manifest themselves. David Howard talks of the fine line that needs to be drawn between pushing a talented child too hard and letting her move so slowly that she loses interest. He has noticed that, when pushed, a child quite often becomes irritable, and sometimes her growth is stunted. He feels this is one reason why some dancers are so small, because all the energy that should be going into growing is going into exercising.

Fiona Fairrie, a former member of the Royal Ballet in London, who has taught in several areas in the United States, talked of a dancer who eventually became a principal with a major ballet company, and who suffered from stunted growth from having been pushed too hard by her mother. She was a trick star who could do sixty-four *fouettés** on stage at the age of fourteen. She had been introduced to the company's class while they were on tour in Los Angeles, and the dancers had resented it, because they wondered why a girl of four feet ten was present when they already felt overcrowded. Everybody ceased wondering when they saw her leg extension, and beautiful instep, and that she could hold one leg high in the air while standing with both hands off the barre. The director of the company said he could not take the child because she was too small but he finally agreed to let her enter the company school, on condition that she was removed from her mother's influence. The girl grew inches in the first year, finally reaching five feet seven inches, and eventually became one of the company's most highly acclaimed dancers.

A talented child is naturally very capable and unless parents are aware of this, there may be no limit to their expectations, as the child will be able to do most things much more easily than the average child. If the parents then push, the problems will start, because they are asking too much to satisfy their own frustrations through their child. One who is treated that way may achieve what her parents want and then have a nervous breakdown.

If a child is talented, she will probably want to build her own path rather than be led along a road that has already been assigned to her, and if she is forced to do something against her will, this will likely prevent the child from using whatever talents or capabilities she may have. Eventually she will probably also resent her parents. The outcome of pushing a child can never be predicted, because even among brothers and sisters who are subjected to the same stresses,

---

* There are many types of fouetté, but here the reference is to the spectacular *fouetté rond de jambe en tournant*: whipped circle of the leg turning. The dancer, "standing on one foot, makes a rapid circular movement with the other leg, thus propelling herself around the supporting leg as an axis, without moving from the spot." The whipping leg should be at hip level, with the foot closing in to the knee of the supporting leg. Fouettés may be executed *en dehors* or *en dedans*. "Fouettés en tournant, done separately from other movements, are performed in series." (The most impressive display of fouettés in all of classical ballet can be seen as performed by the ballerina toward the end of the third act of *Swan Lake*, when thirty-two of them are included in the choreography.) Thirty-two fouettés used to be considered the epitome of achievement, onstage, although now many will do twice that number in class. From *The Dance Encyclopedia*.

some may adjust, while others may not. Everybody has a certain constitution or predisposition, and even the child's position in the family can make a difference.

Lack of stimulation can be stifling for any child, especially a talented one, and one of the worst mistakes a parent can make is to provide no incentives. The most positive contribution that can be made is to follow through when a child shows an interest or talent at a very early age, which might present another set of problems if the child has an inclination to play the drums! The important point is to indulge a child who has an active curiosity and a willingness to try different things. Even a talented person will not be an expert at everything—a great violinist may not know how to fix a car—but that is why the exposure is so important. An active mind needs its stimulation.

There is a great difference between trying to guide a child in a certain direction and imposing one's will upon her. If a child is apathetic about everything, a parent might lead her toward the arts and gently encourage her interest. This takes careful handling because in dealing with a parent-child relationship there is always rebellion going on. First a parent must recognize what is happening in the child's mind, because then he will be able to deal with whatever may be wrong. An adult can accept something of the irrationality of a child's situation, but all too often wants to force that child to overcome her problem rather than take a more rational approach.

Dr. La Manna feels anything that becomes totally consuming is probably a bad thing, but he also feels this is a problem that requires personal advice. It is most important there should be enjoyment from ballet when it is taking so much time in a child's life, and it should not interfere with other pastimes, be they schoolwork or play. If the interest in ballet seems to be becoming an obsession, and the child is obviously not enjoying it, a parent should try communicating with her to find out the reason the child is attempting to "lose" herself in ballet. Should the child be throwing herself into it, it is probably either an escape or a sublimation.

Dr. La Manna warns against the child being allowed to become so absorbed in ballet that her schoolwork suffers, as this is such an important part of her life, and of her future, even if she is working to become a dancer. If she does not achieve her goal, she will need her academic education to give her viable alternatives. Also, whether or not she may like the society she has to move in, she will have to operate within it.

If a child shows a talent for, or a strong interest in, ballet, it is also very important that she be encouraged to pursue her interest without having the feeling that she is in any way different from her peers. A child needs to feel that she is like her friends, and must have that sense of conformity.

The key to a child's balanced outlook is acceptance by the parents. A boy might come home from school and suggest to his father that instead of going to watch football, they go to the ballet. The father's reaction will communicate his attitude to his son, and should he be negative, the boy may well develop the idea that ballet is an interest not to be pursued, for whatever specific reasons his father gives him.

If ballet becomes a child's first love, she will devote a large part of her life to it, take class whenever possible, and probably drive herself endlessly. As she will also have to keep up with a full academic schedule, it probably means she will have very little time to spend with her friends. When they want to play, she will probably prefer to be in class. If she is pursuing a real love this is all right, up to a point.

One thing that Dr. La Manna believes in very strongly is that interests determine who a child will socialize with, rather than the other way around, and this is why, as a child grows up, she may change her circle of friends.

There will always be different demands made on a gifted child and this in turn creates additional pressures. It may not be good enough to learn how to dance, but only to dance very well. This will probably come partly from the parents' pushing and partly from the child. If there is too much pressure, or too much strain, the child will become frustrated and at this point it is very important that the parents are open to discussion. Sometimes for a child to sit down and air her frustration may be all that is needed.

As in all other aspects of the theater, the competition in ballet is extremely tough and a child should be made to realize what she is working toward. If she has the mentality, stamina, and the desire for it, she will work very hard to achieve her ends. Should she be lucky enough to have the talent also, there is a fair chance that she will succeed as a dancer, but with the life being so hard, she should at least be given a choice. She should also be made aware of the sacrifices she will have to make. The hours will be long, the self-discipline required unflagging, and her life will be on a totally different level from most other children. As David Howard remarked, "If a dancer is to succeed in dancing with one of the few good companies in the United States, she must be amongst approximately the top one thousand ballet dancers in the country. If she was a dentist, she would be one of about the top one thousand in the Brooklyn area." Although the statistics on Brooklyn dentists might be somewhat exaggerated, it does effectively illustrate the point.

Psychologist Dr. Albert Ellis, talking about dancers, said, "One forgets that those who get through are the mavericks; they're not average people."

One very positive aspect Dr. La Manna feels about the dance is it gives a child contact with her body and more freedom of movement. Movement can be very therapeutic to an inhibited child, who can then find out that learning to express herself freely is not a devastating process. At Coney Island Hospital experiments have been performed which have shown that body movement is correlated with personality. When there is a disturbance in personality, it is often correlated with disturbance in the body of the child. Dance is one of the techniques used in working with disturbed children, and may even be a means of learning self-control, since music itself is an external control. Some may have a need to adjust their movements to music. At the hospital such experiments in working with children therapeutically have proven extremely successful. This work was done with all from the "normal" child to the seriously disturbed, but not those so seriously disturbed they have to be hospitalized. However, there are many methods that can be used to reach a child or an adult. Dance is but one of them.*

* For those interested in dance as therapy, there is a semiannual publication: *American Jour-*

If a child needs to come to New York to study, there are many matters for a parent to take into consideration. At that age she still needs a family environment, preferably with her parents. If it is not possible for at least one parent to be at hand, then a good family may be found for a child to stay with although this is going to be traumatic to face initially. The competition she will find among the students in the dance schools, together with the pace of life in New York in general, are major problems, especially for a child who is not familiar with big-city life. If the problems presented prove insurmountable, not only will there be little chance of success at dancing but there will also be serious problems generally. For a girl or boy who wishes to come to New York to dance it is probably unwise for either to be alone in the city before the age of eighteen, especially if he or she is far from home.

After several years of training the time will come, inevitably, when some discover they are not going to be able to have careers in ballet.

In this case, if a child has had her heart set on becoming a dancer, she may well become very depressed and unsure of where to turn. Dr. La Manna believes communication between parent and child is the key to overcoming many bad situations, and that it is up to the parent to help rebuild confidence. Dr. Ellis maintains his system of psychotherapy is of paramount importance. He teaches that one always upsets oneself by crooked thinking, and that unhappiness is not caused by people or events. "You have to train an individual from childhood to have a good philosophy of life, which practically no humans have. Many of the dancers, if taught that way, would never become dancers. Those who did go into it would be prepared to take the risk and tell themselves that if they didn't make it, it would be just that simple. That's life." Dr. Ellis also acknowledges how difficult it is to develop this way of thinking, since it is not natural for most humans. "They all whine and scream when they don't get their taffy."

A child should be helped to understand what she is dealing with

nal of Dance Therapy, published and distributed under the auspices of the American Dance Therapy Association, which is in no way responsible for its editorial content. Suite 230, 2000 Century Plaza, Columbia, MD 21044.

the minute it becomes obvious she is taking her dance seriously. On the one hand, she should be able to proceed with the knowledge that if she is prepared to work hard under a good teacher, she has a chance of having a dance career. At the same time, she should know that if she does not become a dancer, there are alternatives in life.

If a talented child is being pushed to succeed in her dancing she may be progressing at a great rate, yet she may not be able to cope with the pressures. There may be a drop-off in areas of performance other than the dance, or there may be a personality change. For example, a happy-go-lucky child may become depressed, or an easygoing child may suddenly become very angry. Another sign that a child is not able to cope is if she is putting progressively more effort into the dance and it is not showing results—the output does not measure up to the input. Alternatively, if a child is capable of devoting tremendous amounts of time to her dance with positive results, then she may well be successful as a dancer. One strong point is she obviously has a sense of how much time is needed if she is to succeed in ballet.

Another thing to be sure of is whether a girl is pursuing the ballet just to please her parents, because the younger the child, the more dependent she will be on them. It is especially important that parents convey the fact that a child should dance only if she enjoys it herself, rather than for their pleasure. A child may have a fear of "losing" her parents if she does not do everything possible to please them, so a girl should be made to feel that she will be supported in whatever positive activity she chooses to pursue.

Mme Darvash talked of the special care needed in raising a talented child, and how crucial it is to pace such a youngster, as with one of her own students. She warned against letting too young a child into a company, feeling that eighteen is appropriate, with independent performing experience being built up from the age of sixteen. Since this particular student was eleven, Madame has kept a careful eye on her progress, for many people are eager to have this young girl perform all over the country. Madame emphasized the great mistake of a dancer's thinking she is ready to perform just because her technique has reached a certain level. "No girl is quite ready to begin performing regularly before about the age of sixteen. She needs many guns for her battle. She should study acting and learn how to interpret musical phrasing, and this takes the extra years. It is bad to constantly remind a child how talented she is, because it not only builds up her hopes unrealistically, but it makes people expect too much of her. Finally, she should not be allowed to make repeated appearances just to show off, because this can be ruinous emotionally."

As if echoing Mme Darvash's words, there is a sign sitting on her desk, given to her by one of her students: "No one ever said it was going to be easy. But this is ridiculous!"

EIGHT

The Boy in Dance

In our highly categorized society, if a boy is to take ballet classes, he needs moral support and encouragement. Until very recently, most boys who decided they wanted to study ballet were virtually asking to be ostracized by their friends, and many of them were. Some would even go to great lengths to hide the fact, because they were afraid of being labeled sissies.

Fortunately, for the most part, the world is now more aware. Maybe it is due in some degree to the pioneering and hard work of Erik Bruhn and Rudolf Nureyev, who both determined to show the world they deserved as much attention as their female counterparts. At this stage, they are being followed by countless others who wanted to be dancers and who are impressing audiences everywhere as the outstanding male dancers of our time, such as Mikhail Baryshnikov, Anthony Dowell, Peter Martins, Richard Cragun, Peter Schaufuss, and Fernando Bujones. Among other equally fine exponents were Ivan Nagy, recently retired, and Edward Villella, who now makes limited appearances. There is still a critical shortage of good male ballet dancers, but, fortunately, boys are appearing in ever-increasing numbers at the dance studios. The days when boys were automatically given scholarships have passed, at least in New York, although until very recently the dance world was actually that desperate to have them. So critical was the shortage, one even wonders, if press-ganging had not been outlawed, whether dance company directors and teachers would not have been seen with cloak and dagger in the night, abducting boy recruits to train as ballet dancers. However, nowadays not only is the idea of men in ballet catching on, it is actually spreading.

In Ithaca, New York, Barbara Thuesen announced happily that

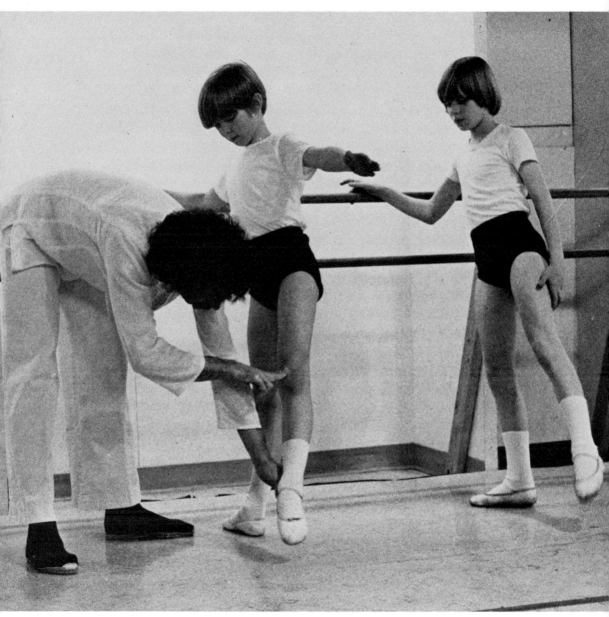

Frank Bourman explains turnout to young boys at the School of the Minnesota Dance Theatre. The growing child must learn from the beginning the correct way to stretch the leg and foot.
Photo: Joseph Ketola

she now has a class of some half-dozen fourteen-year-old boys. They decided to take up ballet since, loving ballet skiing,* they felt it would help their balance. Whether or not a ballet career is the ultimate aim, or ballet training is used simply to supplement some other form of activity, it is significant that ballet for men is beginning to be recognized for its many advantages, rather than ridiculed. With these particular boys, it all began because one of them wanted to take ballet, and his friends decided to try it also.

Films such as *Turning Point*, in which Mikhail Baryshnikov gave a bravura performance, no doubt influenced some boys—and probably their parents also. Television presentations that feature the great male dancers of many fine ballet companies throughout the United States and Europe have possibly provided inspiration for those boys contemplating taking ballet classes, and maybe even changed the notions of those who were once of the confirmed belief they would never show an interest in an activity in which tights were the uniform.

Edward Villella, a principal with New York City Ballet, once gave a lecture-demonstration, which was captured on film,† at the Brooklyn high school from which he was graduated. As he walked onstage, he was greeted by titters from the teenage boys. When he began to talk about ballet, they exchanged remarks behind their hands and many had smirks on their faces. Mr. Villella had to work hard. He told them how he had won his letters in football at high school and college, and talked of football in terms they could relate to ballet. After only a few minutes, he had begun to convince them of what it takes to be a male ballet dancer: the strength of a weight lifter, combined with the maximum amount of grace and artistry—an artistic athlete. Mr. Villella then danced, together with Patricia McBride, who had accompanied him from the New York City Ballet, and the

---

*Adaptation of ballet steps that are feasible on skiis.

†*Man Who Dances: Edward Villella, 1968*, A.T.&T. Telecast on the "Bell Telephone Hour," NBC-TV, March 8, 1968. Produced by Robert Drew and Mike Jackson.

Men's class at the North Carolina School of the Arts in which they demonstrate *relevé en seconde* (second position), with the arms in fifth.

Photo: Michael Avedon

attitude of the boys in the audience changed, one by one. The talking stopped. The shuffling ceased. Their attention was held. The room full of tittering schoolboys turned into one filled with wide-eyed, admiring young men. The demonstration finished, they reacted with whistles and loud applause.

With such social stigma having been attached to men in ballet, many of them were not able to dance while young. Some were not allowed to study ballet, but even more of them were probably never even exposed to the art. David Howard thinks this causes a great shortage of boys entering ballet at the right age. As he said, "They tend to start when they're about to go on Social Security!" He regrets seeing men starting at the age of twenty. Sometimes they have everything going for them: good bodies, good muscle alignment, musicality, sensitivity, and good looks, but their parents never allowed them to take ballet. Then it becomes a real challenge to see how much can be accomplished. Some turn out to be totally uncoordinated and seem to go across the floor as though they have both legs tied together, but it is often those men who are the most persistent because they want to dance so badly.

On rare occasions boys start ballet at the age of seventeen or eighteen and still become professional enough, after about two years of training, to be accepted by one of the companies. This is due to the shortage of men, especially in the regional companies. Realistically it takes about five years to train a boy to become a classical ballet dancer. When starting late, a boy should keep in mind that basic barre technique is essential for development and can be achieved only with a proficient teacher and constant personal attention. He should take two classes a day and practice enough on his own to spend about six hours training each day.

As a boy, Mr. Howard was never trained with girls, and regrets the fact, because without them the teacher's undivided attention is on the boys. Once a boy has entered ballet class he needs to be made to feel special because of the social problems he has to overcome, but there again it is necessary to keep a good balance because he must not be made to feel too special. If a boy does study in a class that includes girls, it will be at the stage that the girls go into pointe work that the boys will put extra concentration into double tours, *entrechat-six*,* and traveling steps.† While the girls are simply learning to go up and down on pointe, the boys will need time spent with them individually also, as they work on their double tours. The timing works well, and the teacher is kept very active.

A boy's training is basically the same as that of a girl—minus the pointe work, although some do take pointe class as it strengthens the feet. This is why, as David Howard explained, boys are often better at jumping than girls, because while a girl is putting time and effort into her pointe work, a boy is able to practice the virtuoso steps, such as brisés volés and cabrioles.

Certain teachers include all-male classes in their schedules, and on these occasions they concentrate on the virtuoso steps, which is also the reason why one or two girls may attend. These classes will run the same length as those that are mixed.

For a boy to be granted a scholarship in most schools, he must show a degree of aptitude, but boys in ballet classes are still considerably outnumbered by girls, which gives them an obvious advantage. As Jody Fugate, who teaches at the Mme Darvash Ballet School, states, "Girls undergo much more pressure because the competition among them is so much greater."

It is true that girls have to pedal harder than boys to reach the same destination. "Consequently," added Ms. Fugate, "the standard is much higher among girls than boys, generally speaking."

The First U.S.A. International Ballet Competition, which took place in Jackson, Mississippi, in June 1979, presented a challenge to that. In the *New York Times*, Jennifer Dunning mentioned Koenraad Onzia, a seventeen-year-old Belgian, "whose elegant line and polished technique won him the top junior division medal. All agreed that male competition far outshone the women in this age of the male dancer."

---

*"A movement in which the dancer crosses his legs repeatedly while in the air. . . . The number following the word entrechat indicates the movements of each leg." From *The Dance Encyclopedia*.

†Any steps or combination of steps in which the dancer moves from one position to another across the floor.

In fact, though Mr. Onzia and twenty-three-year-old Lubomir Kafka of Czechoslovakia won the top medals at the competition, no gold medals were awarded to the women. Of the three men who won silver medals, two of them were from the United States, as were three of the six bronze medal winners.

When a boy has reached the level of training at which he is ready to enter a company, in New York his chances are fairly even with those of a girl. This is simply because, although there are more girls in most companies at the corps de ballet level, there are also more of them competing for those places. At both American Ballet Theatre and New York City Ballet the numbers tend to be approximately equal at the soloist level, and at present, both companies have more principal men than women. At the Joffrey Ballet Company, where the dancers are not categorized, the scales tip slightly in favor of men.

Advanced men's class at the San Francisco Ballet School in which the students are doing a variation on *attitude croisé derrière*.
Photo: Fred Morales, Jr.

Outside New York a boy's chances of entering a company will almost certainly be greater than those of a girl.

David Howard says most of the injuries experienced by men are chiefly in the neck and lower back. They also tend to be more prone to knee injuries. The reason the neck usually suffers is the result of a

Former Bolshoi Ballet principal Andrei Kramarevsky passes on his expertise to the advanced men's class at the School of American Ballet. *Photo: Steven Caras*

man's lifting a woman on to one of his shoulders and moving around with her in that position. On such occasions, the head is forced to one side, which puts the spine out of alignment, and this can eventually lead to problems. The lower back injuries are caused by lifts, and nowadays many men take special exercises, other than ballet, to help build extra strength in the back muscles and so help to prevent injuries in that area. These exercises are definitely recommended. Knee injuries are caused by the excessive stress of jumping.

It seems the days when boys were afraid to admit they even showed an interest in ballroom dancing have passed, as now they all hurl themselves through the movements of disco dancing. With it, boys are showing up in ever-increasing numbers to study ballet.

NINE

Adult Beginner Classes

The popularity of the ballet class is not limited to aspiring dancers. There is now an age group that is mainly pursuing ballet for totally different reasons—the adult beginners. These people are flocking to ballet schools in such numbers that, in some of the well-known studios, students have to be turned away.

A great many studios, other than those major schools that feed companies directly, are now giving adult beginner classes. Some that have been running these classes for a few years have found they have beginners who needed to be upgraded and for whom they have added intermediate classes.

These beginner classes are interesting because of the variety of people they are encouraging—people as varied as their reasons for studying ballet. Some are in class because they took ballet as children and after many years away have been drawn back to it, if only for the exercise. Maybe they are there because they have put on weight and believe ballet will slim them down, which it probably will do if combined with the right diet. Some have an air about them that says their prime interest is to let go as they leap across the floor, watching themselves in the mirror, and seeing not their own images but those of their favorite stars. They indulge themselves for a few minutes in class, so the next time they see their favorites taking the bows, the curtain calls, and the flowers, they are able to identify in some small degree.

In class at David Howard's school, there is a man of thirty-five, an ex-navy pilot, and currently an architect, who is taking class every day in the hope of being accepted by a company. As Douglas Wassell told him candidly, "You must realize all the odds are against you, but what is important is you have determination and what you are doing makes you happy. However, it is only fair to be realistic with you." The man understood the situation. "I appreciate your honesty, and I realize what you are saying," he replied. "After all, here am I trying to get into a company just at the age when most men are thinking about retiring."

The ballet season in New York is now year round, and during the summer months there are, more often than not, two or three major ballet companies dancing at any one time. It has reached the point where some international companies occasionally have to miss out on New York altogether, simply because the suitable houses are already fully booked, as the city proudly plays host as dance capital of the world. The conversation in the changing rooms at the dance classes often revolves around whichever company is appearing, and opinions and comparisons are offered. As usual on such occasions (and it is the same in the standing-room lines at Lincoln Center), the adulation is great—and the criticism severe. For many of these people, ballet plays an important part in life.

Those who study as adults follow many different occupations. There are secretaries, doctors, visual artists, athletes, teachers, lawyers, computer programmers, writers, social workers, singers, actors, students, and housewives, to name some of them. There are those in their late teens, and those of an age as high as stamina and determination will allow in a ballet class. It is not unusual to see people in their forties and even fifties among the beginners.

Although some classes may be given by teachers who just want to put their students through an easy exercise class and collect the cash, this certainly is not true at the good schools, and these are the ones to stay with. Usually a school that has good professional classes will be good at the beginner level also. Here classes are taken very seriously by both teachers and students, and they are *very* hard work. Beginner classes are known to be the hardest because of their preciseness and the slow pace at which the exercises are given. Occasionally professional dancers will appear in such a class given by their own teacher, especially during a time when they are doing a great deal of heavy performing, because even they develop bad habits. This happens rather in the way that it does with most automobile drivers once they have obtained their licenses. Although the overall expertise and knowledge are there, those little habits that make life easier inevitably creep in.

The point to emphasize is these classes are ballet classes and require the same amount of hard work as ballet does on any level. If they are not hard, they are not good classes, and will only be a waste of time for the students. For many adults there is the added problem of loss of pliability and muscles that have become weak through inactivity, so to tone and stretch them takes extra energy.

These adult beginner classes are both serving a useful purpose and filling a growing need. As society comes closer to ballet, more people are pursuing that interest by involving themselves in the basic elements of the art.

The Professional

Once having read this book, the reader should feel confident about forming an opinion on any ballet class he or she may consider, whether as parent, or adult beginner. The physical aspects of a class and the educational abilities of a teacher are points that can be measured. What cannot be measured is the desire of a person to take ballet, her reasons for wanting to be involved, or the degree of talent and determination she has to make her succeed. These will only come to light over a long period of time. Natalia Makarova has this advice to give the young dancer. "Always keep looking forward to find stimulation and excitement, for the artist who stops searching stops growing. It is very important to find one's own depth and never to be superficial or shallow. Still I find myself thinking about something new every day, something I've never thought before."

One very important aspect that cannot be ignored is the power of the theater as a wooer. She is indeed a powerful seductress, demanding a great deal of those who pursue her, and giving small return to most and riches and fame beyond the dreams of most to only a very few. Thus, it is not so much whether a person wants to pursue a dance career, but whether she is psychologically equipped to deal with the problems should she not succeed. Unless she has been forced into it, any child who goes to ballet class, and who seems to have her heart set on becoming a dancer once she grows up, is probably living for the day she will be part of a company, hoping to work her way to the top.

What should be noted is that most of the people in the companies are not dancing to become rich or famous—though both these aspects are usually welcome if they do transpire. The majority of dancers realize the truth and occasional heartbreak involved in their daily lives.

There is probably not a ballet dancer on the stage anywhere who would say she is in the profession for the glamor. It is not glamorous to have to get up at ten o'clock in the morning with an aching body from the night before, in order to rush to class at eleven o'clock, to push that body through more hard work. It is not glamorous to be called in the event of an emergency, and be given a few hours of rehearsal (if you are lucky) and then have to perform that same night. It is not glamorous to be told after a day's traveling that a person who was supposed to be doing a particular part is for some reason not able to do it and, without being mentally prepared, having to appear onstage. It is even less glamorous having to keep up this pace for weeks, even months, on end, knowing an injury could take weeks to recover from and the more tired the body as the season progresses, the greater the chance of that injury happening.

The pluses are to be found by those who really want to be dancers—they will have the chance to enjoy what they love most—and that is to dance. It is the way dancers express themselves best and for some it is the only form of expression in which they can really let themselves go. Once on stage, they are cut off from the rest of the world. There is nothing that exists beyond the curtain. The people to whom they relate are the other dancers onstage around them, and in character roles they are relating to people who are as removed from reality at that moment as they are themselves. They are all living their fantasies together in a way most people can only imagine. They can escape within their characterization, and in the abstract ballets, they go onstage with the idea of giving their all to fulfill the technical demands. Following a good performance, they will float home. After a bad one, or just making a mistake that throws them off, they may cry for two days.

It is wonderful to watch those who do work hard and consistently climb the ladder, to see them be given more and more important roles until they become soloists, and eventually maybe principals. Although those who are the most highly successful are to be respected and admired, there are countless other dancers whose names never hit the lights who are a delight to watch in their specific roles.

People who want to dance badly enough will pursue their chosen art and give it everything they have to be successful. Just as it is probably not good to hold back the children who have that goal in mind, so it is probably no better to force those who do not. The former will probably be miserable without it and the latter will probably suffer every day of their lives if pushed.

The glamor is in the eyes of the onlooker. The best chance for self-fulfillment is in the heart and mind of the dancer who as she looks at the rest of the world says to herself, "I like to keep score. With ballet, I know who's ahead."

In summary: ballet is very hard work, from the day a child first enters the classroom to the day she ends her career. It is crucial that she receive the best training, if she is to have any hope at all of being accepted by a company. Although ballet is becoming more widespread throughout the United States, the standard is also rising and every year the competition grows stiffer.

It is not possible to gauge the percentage of those who are successful, since many dancers may start their training in one city and move to another, or even stay in the same city but change teachers. However, one thing is certain. The percentage of students who are eventually accepted into the companies is very small. The majority, once dancing, do not make it beyond the corps de ballet level. It is only the occasional dancer, with exceptional talent, who graduates to soloist before several years have passed, and some remain in the corps for about ten years before being promoted. After that, they may or may not become principals, since it takes exceptional artistry as well as good technique for a dancer to be promoted to that most illustrious rank.

For those who survive a full ballet career, the years as a dancer pass quickly. Most men retire by the age of forty, some by thirty-five, or even younger, since the wear and tear on the body prevents them from continuing any longer. In some cases a career will be finished early by a major injury. The majority of women either retire or, at least, are dancing considerably less by the time they have reached the age of forty.

Consequently it is wise for those who need to support themselves, and maybe families, to plan for alternative occupations, whether or not such occupations are dance related.

Those with the talent, stamina, desire, and ability to work hard consider there are no alternatives as long as they can dance. Certainly they are to be encouraged, not only for the fulfillment they themselves enjoy but also for the joy they bring to others through their dancing.

NAMES AND CREDENTIALS OF TEACHERS
INTERVIEWED FOR THIS BOOK

(listed alphabetically under schools)

American Ballet Center (official school
  of the Joffrey Ballet)
434 Avenue of the Americas
New York, NY 10011
Tel.: (212) 254–8520
N.B. At the time of going to press, this
  school had officially changed its name
  to the Joffrey Ballet School.

MEREDITH BAYLIS
trained:
  Mme Nijinska, Michael Panaeff,
    Mme Swoboda
danced with:
  Ballet Russe de Monte Carlo; reached rank
    of soloist
teaching affiliation:
  American Ballet Center since 1965
  Head of the Scholarship Program

BASIL THOMPSON
trained:
  Sadlers Wells School, England
danced with:
  Royal Ballet, England; later American
    Ballet Theatre soloist
teaching affiliations:
  Joffrey Ballet, ballet master 1967–76
  American Ballet Center, 1976–1979
  New Jersey Ballet Company, ballet master
    since December 1979

American Ballet Theatre School
3 West 61 Street
New York, NY 10023
Tel.: (212) 586–3355
N.B. At the time of going to press, this
  school was searching for new premises.

PATRICIA WILDE
trained:
  Canada (Russian school); School of
    American Ballet, London and Paris

danced with:
  Marquis de Cuevas Company
  Ballet Russe de Monte Carlo
  Roland Petit Company
  New York City Ballet (principal)
other:
  first Director Harkness Ballet
  currently Director, American Ballet
    Theatre School
teaching affiliations:
  New York City Ballet
  School of American Ballet
  American Ballet Theatre (ballet mistress)
  American Ballet Theatre School—currently
  Dance Theatre of Harlem—currently

Fiona Fairrie
trained:
  Royal Ballet School
danced with:
  Royal Ballet, England
  Stuttgart Ballet
choreographed for:
  many schools and companies throughout
    the United States
teaching affiliations:
  several schools, including Washington,
    D.C., Atlanta, Georgia, and
    Chattanooga, Tennessee

David Howard School of Ballet
36 West 62 Street
New York, NY 10023
Tel.: (212) 757–9877

DAVID HOWARD
trained:
  George Gontcheroav (great Russian
    teacher) and others
danced with:
  Sadlers Wells Ballet (later Royal Ballet),
    England

National Ballet of Canada
appeared in a Royal Command
    Performance before Her Majesty Queen
    Elizabeth II
awards include:
    Royal Academy of Dancing's highest
        honor—the Adeline Genee Medal
    John F. Kennedy Freedom Foundation
        Award
other credits:
    numerous, including choreographic.
    National Association for Regional Ballet—
        president
    adjudicator for American contestants for
        First American International Ballet
        Competition, Jackson, Mississippi, June
        1979
    has cut four teaching record albums
teaching affiliations:
    Harkness Ballet Company
    Harkness Ballet School (became Director)
    own school since September 1977

DOUGLAS WASSELL
trained:
    Michigan
    North Carolina School of the Arts
    American Ballet Theatre School
        (scholarship student)
    Harkness Ballet School
danced with:
    Les Grands Ballet Canadiens
teaching affiliations include:
    American Ballet Center (Joffrey School)
    Harkness Ballet School
    David Howard School of Ballet since
        opening (September 1977)

ANNE HEBARD
Although not interviewed, Ms. Hebard has
recently begun teaching at the David
Howard School of Ballet. Trained in
England, she holds the R.A.D. Advanced
Certificate with Honours as well as the
Cecchetti and Imperial Society of Teachers
of Dancing examinations.

School of Cleveland Ballet
Stouffer Building Suite 110
1375 Euclid Avenue
Cleveland, OH 44115
Tel.: (216) 621–3633

DENNIS NAHAT
trained:
    Detroit
    Juilliard School of Music (scholarship
        student)
danced with:
    American Ballet Theatre
    Joffrey Ballet
choreographic credits include:
    American Ballet Theatre
    Royal Swedish Ballet
    London Festival Ballet
    Cleveland Ballet
other experience:
    many other credits, including appearing in
        film version of his own ballet, *Some
        Times*, at American Ballet Theatre.
        Conducted seminars in choreography
        throughout the United States for the
        National Association for Regional Ballet
teaching affiliations:
    Cleveland Ballet (Company and School)

Mme Darvash Ballet Studio, Ltd.
1845 Broadway at 60 Street
New York, NY 10019
Tel.: (212) 265–5608

GABRIELA TAUB-DARVASH
trained:
    at private school in Timişoara, Rumania,
        then Opera Ballet School
    The Vaganova School, Leningrad
    Lunatcharski University of Performing
        Arts in Moscow (there studied
        choreography with Leonid Lavrovsky)
performing experience:
    started performing with the local company
        in Timişoara at sixteen and remained
        there for three years

other experience:

Rumania State Opera at Cluj—principal choreographer and ballet director

many other credits, including resident choreographer with Garden State Ballet, New Jersey

currently artistic director of the State Ballet of Connecticut

teaching affiliations include:

State School of Ballet in Cluj

Israeli Ballet Company

Bat Dor Ballet Company, Tel Aviv

Metropolitan Opera Ballet Company

Garden State Ballet, New Jersey

State Ballet of Connecticut

own school since 1975

JODY FUGATE

training:

School of Garden State Ballet, Newark, New Jersey

Southern Connecticut State College

danced with:

Garden State Ballet

Greater Bridgeport Ballet Company

other experience:

ballet mistress, Garden State Ballet

Greater Bridgeport Ballet

Ballet Galaxy 1979

teaching affiliations include:

School of Garden State Ballet

master classes in New York for Professional Dance Teachers' Association in 1977

Mme Darvash Ballet Studio since 1978

NORA KOVACH

Although not interviewed, Mme Kovach also teaches at the Mme Darvash Ballet Studio. Trained in Budapest, Hungary, she became the star of the Budapest Opera. With her partner, Istvan Rabovsky, she was the first ever foreign dancer to appear on stage with the Kirov Ballet after the Soviet Revolution. She was coached privately by Vaganova for eight months, and has danced all over the world with the leading ballet companies. Mme Kovach also works at Mme Darvash Ballet Studio as a coach.

Joffrey Ballet School (see American Ballet Center)

School of American Ballet (official school of the New York City Ballet)

144 West 66th Street

New York, NY 10023

Tel.: (212) 877–0600

ALEXANDRA DANILOVA

trained:

Imperial (now Soviet State) Ballet School, Leningrad

danced with:

Maryinsky Theatre (debut)

Diaghilev Ballet (ballerina)

Col. de Basil's Ballets Russes (ballerina)

Ballet Russe de Monte Carlo (prima ballerina)

headed own group 1954–56

staged ballets:

Metropolitan Opera, New York

La Scala, Milan

Washington Ballet

Hamburg Ballet

teaching affiliation:

School of American Ballet since September 1964

ANDREI KRAMAREVSKY

trained:

Moscow Choreographic Institute

danced with:

Bolshoi Ballet Company (principal)

teaching affiliation:

School of American Ballet since March 1976

Barbara Thuesen

trained:

several teachers including Oleg Tupine and Alexandra Danilova

dance credits:
> has appeared in concerts throughout the United States

other experience:
> has created and developed dance organizations throughout the United States; also choreographs and writes

teaching affiliations:
> extensive list of credits, including organizations she created. Currently, Tompkins County Center for Culture and the Performing Arts, Inc., Ithaca, New York

Although the teachers interviewed for this book have fine reputations, it should be noted that there are dozens of teachers throughout the United States who are equally reputable. In New York City alone there are other highly regarded teachers at the American Ballet Center, American Ballet Theatre School, and the School of American Ballet; others have schools of their own.

List of Additional Ballet Schools

Some other currently reputable schools in the United States and Canada that may be contacted for details of their classes are listed here. Some take child beginners, others require previous training. Many are official company schools. (They are listed alphabetically by state.)

CALIFORNIA

Stanley Holden Dance Center
10521 West Pico Boulevard
Los Angeles, CA 90064

Los Angeles Ballet
11843 West Olympic Boulevard
Los Angeles, CA 90064

San Francisco Ballet School
378 18th Avenue
San Francisco, CA 94121

GEORGIA

Atlanta School of Ballet
3215 Cains Hill Place, NW
Atlanta, GA 30305

ILLINOIS

National Academy of Dance
17 East University Avenue
Champaign, IL 61820

Stone Camryn School of Ballet
185 West Madison Street
Chicago, IL 60602

LOUISIANA

Giacobbe Academy of Dance
6925 Veterans Boulevard
Metairie, LA 70001

MASSACHUSETTS

Boston Ballet
19 Clarendon Street
Boston, MA 02116

MINNESOTA

Minnesota Dance Theatre & School
528 Hennepin Avenue
Room 605
Minneapolis, MN 55403

NORTH CAROLINA

North Carolina School of the Arts
200 Waughtown Street
Post Office Box 12189
Winston-Salem, NC 27107

OHIO

Schwarz School of the Dance
140 North Main Street
Dayton, OH 45402

PENNSYLVANIA

Pennsylvania Ballet
2333 Fairmount Avenue
Philadelphia, PA 19130

TEXAS

High School for Performing and Visual Arts
3517 Austin Street
Houston, TX 77004

Texas Christian University
Division of Ballet and Modern Dance
P.O. Box 30270A
Fort Worth, TX 76129

UTAH

Ballet West
P.O. Box 11336
Salt Lake City, UT 84147

WASHINGTON, D.C.

Washington Ballet
3515 Wisconsin Avenue
Washington, DC 20016

WASHINGTON STATE

Ballet Tacoma
$902^1/_2$ North 2nd
Tacoma, WA 98403

Dorothy Fisher Concert Dancers
9715 Firdale Avenue
Edmonds, WA 98020

Pacific North West Ballet School
4649 Sunnyside Avenue North
Seattle, WA 98103

CANADA

Les Grands Ballet Canadiens
5465 Queen Mary Road
Montreal
Quebec, Canada H3X 1V5

National Ballet of Canada
157 King Street East
Toronto
Ontario, Canada M5C 1G9

Royal Winnipeg Ballet
289 Portage Avenue
Winnipeg
Manitoba, Canada R3B 2B4

SPECIALIST ORGANIZATIONS

For specific information on examinations, ballet conferences, seminars, summer schools, and other important programs, the following organizations (see Styles, pp. 32–36) may be contacted:

Cecchetti Council of America
c/o Jane Caryl Miller
770 Greenhills Drive
Ann Arbor, MI 48105

Miss Elaine Keller
Executive Secretary
Royal Academy of Dancing
8 College Avenue
Upper Montclair, NJ 07043
Tel.: (201) 746-0184

International Summer School
London, England

Bournonville
Registrar
Ballet West
P.O. Box 8745
Aspen, CO 81611

International Summer School
Copenhagen, Denmark

SOME MANUFACTURERS
AND SUPPLIERS OF BALLET WEAR

Capezio
755 Seventh Avenue
New York, NY 10019
Tel.: (212) 245–2130
(Shops in more than forty cities in the
   United States)

Frederick Freed Ltd. of London
108 West 57 Street
New York, NY 10019
Tel.: (212) 489–1055

Gamba distributor:
Tantara
19 Christopher Street
New York, NY 10014
Tel.: (212) 242–7196
(This is just one of many distributors
   throughout the United States and is a
   distributor *only*, not a wholesale supplier.)

Gamba Manufacturer's Headquarters:
5 Northfield Park Industrial Estate
Beresford Avenue
Wembley, Middlesex HAO 1GW
England

Selva & Sons, Inc.
47–25 34 Street
Long Island City, NY 11101
Tel.: (212) 786–1234

All the above manufacturers distribute widely and advertise regularly in *Dancemagazine*, where they list their outlets in the United States.

GLOSSARY

Adagio *See* Temps d'adagio.

Allegro *See* Temps d'allegro.

American Ballet Center Official school of the Joffrey Ballet Company.

Attitude A pose wherein one leg is raised at the back, well bent at the knee. Usually the same arm as leg is raised. In front attitude the working leg is raised in front, knee slightly bent, opposite arm raised. In both cases, foot is held parallel to or slightly below the knee. When the term attitude is used without alternative qualification, it is automatically assumed that the working leg is to the back.

Batterie A generic term applied to all movements in which the feet beat together or one foot beats against the other.

Body (on the) No position should be superimposed on any physique. The student should learn to use the leeway that exists, to suit her own body type, even in classical positions.

Brisés volés Flying brisés, literally, broken movements. A series of jumps requiring very difficult and complex movements of the legs and feet.

Cabriole A movement in the air in which the legs are at an angle to the floor and the lower leg beats against the upper leg.

Chaîné Chain, link. In the plural, abbreviation of *tours chaînés déboulés*: a series of rapid turns on pointes or demi-pointes done in a straight line or a circle.

Coda The third part of the classic pas de deux, which follows the variations. In it the male and the female dancer are on the stage together. They alternate in their dances, but finish the coda together. Alternatively, the finale of a classic ballet in which all principals appear separately or with their partners. (A good example of a coda is the mazurka finale in *The Sleeping Beauty*.)

Couru Running.

Demi-pointe Half-pointe (up on the ball of the foot).

Dessous Under. Indicates that the working foot passes behind the supporting foot.

Dessus Over. Indicates that the working foot passes in front of the supporting foot.

Double tour en l'air Two turns in the air.

Effaceé Pose of the body when it is at an angle to the audience and working leg is extended away from the body, not crossing it in the spectator's line of vision.

Enchaînement Linking. A combination of two or more steps arranged to fit a phrase of music.

En dedans A term used to describe inward circular movements of the legs or arms, such as *fouetté en dedans*. Compare with *en dehors*.

En dehors   A term used to describe
outward circular movement of the legs or
arms, such as *fouetté en dehors*. Compare
with *en dedans*.

En tournant   Turning. Indicates that the
body is to turn while executing a given
step.

Entrechat-six   A movement in which the
dancer crosses his legs repeatedly while in
the air. The number following the word
entrechat indicates the movements of each
leg.

Épaulement   The use of the shoulders in
presenting a step to the audience. Indicates
the movement of the torso from the waist
upward, bringing one shoulder forward
and the other back with the head turned
or inclined over the forward shoulder.

Fouetté   There are many types of fouetté,
but here the reference is to the spectacular
fouetté rond de jambe en tournant: literally,
whipped circle of the leg turning. The
dancer, standing on one foot, makes a
rapid circular movement with the other
leg, thus propelling herself around the
supporting leg as an axis without moving
from the spot. The whipping leg should be
at hip level, with the foot closing in to the
knee of the supporting leg. Fouettés may
be executed *en dehors* or *en dedans*. *Fouettés en
tournant*, done separately from other
movements, are performed in a series.

Frog position   Placing of the bottoms of the
feet together with heels pulled in toward
the pelvis.

Glissade   A gliding step; preparatory
movement for leaps.

Hyperextension   A condition where the
knee joint drops back.

Placement   Good alignment of legs in terms
of turnout (hip rotation); good posture; all
lines coming from the body correct

according to the required position.

Plié   A bending of the knee or knees.

Pointe   (the toe)   The position of the foot
in which there is a continuous line from
the toe on which the dancer stands,
through the instep, ankle, knee, and hip.
In dance, pointe work is unique to women
in ballet.

Port de bras   Movement of the arms.

Roll-in (or Roll-out)   When the ankles drop
inward (or outward).

Rosin   The translucent, brittle resin left
after distilling the turpentine from the
crude resin of the pine. Used by ballet
dancers on their shoes to prevent them
from slipping on floors and stages.

School of American Ballet   Official school
of the New York City Ballet.

Sickle   A technical fault in which the foot
is turned over, either inward or outward,
from the ankle, thus breaking the line of
the leg.

Sleepers   Heavy, horizontal timbers placed
under wood floors for distributing loads.

Temps d'adagio   In this sense, a series of
exercises during a ballet lesson designed to
develop grace, a sense of line, and balance,
and done to slow music.

Temps d'allegro   As used here, part of the
lesson which follows the adagio, the
jumps, batterie, and turns done to a fast or
moderate tempo.

Tour   A turn.

Traveling steps   Any steps or combination
of steps in which the dancer moves from
one position to another across the floor.

Turnout   Outward rotation in the hip
joints.

Variation   As used here, the second part of
the classic pas de deux following the
adagio (combination of steps done to slow
music). Invariably a solo.

NOTE: Most definitions of ballet terms are taken from *The Dance Encyclopedia,* rev. and enl.,
compiled and edited by Anatole Chujoy and P. W. Manchester (Simon & Schuster, 1967) and
from *Technical Manual and Dictionary of Classical Ballet* by Gail Grant (Dover Publications, 1967).

The following terms, occurring in captions, apply specifically to the positions and movements in the accompanying photographs.

Arabesque Possibly the most widely known of ballet poses, in which one leg with the foot pointed is extended to the back at right angles to the supporting leg. The standing leg may be on pointe, demi-pointe, or the whole foot, and either straight or demi-plié. There are many forms of arabesque in which the position of the arms and body vary.

  face à la barre Facing the barre.

  relevé sur demi-pointe (first position) In which the foot of the supporting leg is raised on demi-pointe.

Arrière, en Backward. In which a step is executed in that direction, away from the audience.

Attitude

  croisé derrière Crossed attitude. The dancer stands facing one of the front corners of the stage, with the standing leg nearer the audience.

  en demi-plié Supporting leg half bent.

Avant, en Forward. In which a step is executed in that direction, toward the audience.

Croisé Crossed. The body is at an oblique angle to the audience and the working leg crosses the line of the body either in front or behind it.

Demi-plié Knee or knees half bent.

Devant In front.

Développé écarté A movement in which the working leg is drawn up before being extended in the air and held with perfect control. The dancer faces one of the front corners of the stage.

Jeté en avant, grand A large jump forward from one leg to the other, in which the working leg is swept into the air as if thrown.

Passé Passed. The working leg is raised to the side with the knee bent and the foot pointed downward. The pointe brushes against the standing leg to knee level in front and is then passed down immediately behind it so that the foot is returned to its original position on the floor. It can also be done with the working leg moving from the back to the front.

  sur pointe en écarté On pointe, executed facing one of the front corners of the stage.

Penché en avant en sous-sus Leaning forward with the body raised on pointes in the fifth position. The dancer springs onto the pointes making sure that the legs and feet are tightly together, heels forward, giving the impression of one foot when viewed from the front.

Quatrième Fourth. Referring to the fourth of the five classical positions of the feet.

Relevé Raised. The body is raised on pointe or pointes, demi-pointe or demi-pointes.

  en seconde Second. The dancer is on pointe with the working leg raised to the side of the body, or second position.

  sur pointe en seconde arabesque On pointe in second arabesque.

  sur les pointes en première On pointes in the first position.

Tendu Stretched.

INDEX

BALLET SCHOOL EVALUATION CHECKLIST

FACILITY	EXCELLENT	GOOD	FAIR	POOR
Floor				
Materials and pliability/surface				
Studio size				
Height				
Mirrors				
Barre				
Temperature				

TEACHER				
Personal appearance				
Carriage/walk				
Knowledge of anatomy				
Knowledge of French terminology				
Extensiveness of ballet vocabulary				
Credentials/dance conventions former dancer				
Sense of humor/sensitivity				
Possessiveness				

CLASSES				
Discipline				
Length				
Organization				
Floor work				
Barre				
Center				
Style/syllabus				
Size (number of students)				
Frequency				

STUDENTS				
Dress				
Body				
Feet				
Pointe work (if applicable)				
Enjoyment				